Guide to
Child Protection Mediation

(Second Edition)

By:
Paul James Brown

© 2018 Paul James Brown
paulbrownmediation.com

All rights reserved. No part of this publication may be reproduced, distributed, stored in a retrieval system, or transmitted in any form by any process – electronic, mechanical, photocopying, recording, or otherwise – without the prior written permission of the author.

Published By: Paul James Brown
Edited By: Nick Halmasy, MACP, Registered Psychotherapist
  Stephanie Rudd, B Comm, J.D.
Cover Design By: Jeff Tidd of JET Media
Paul Brown Mediation Logo Design By: Leslee Uddenberg

Printed in Canada and the United States of America by Lulu Press Inc.

ISBN 978-1-387-60041-0 (paperback)
ISBN 978-1-387-66924-0 (e-book)

Author's Note:
All of the stories and/ or examples in this book are based on actual experiences. The names may have been changed to protect the privacy of the people involved.

This book is dedicated to the clients we serve. That includes workers, lawyers, and most importantly, families. My hope is that by Mediators, Child Welfare Specialists, and Community Service Providers reading this book, it will help level the playing field so that we provide a better service to our families.

Helping families is why we do this work... PJB

FOREWORD

Before she became a judge, Madam Justice June Maresca was my primary mentor when I was learning to become a family mediator. At that time she was pioneering something new in Ontario; the idea of using mediation to empower families and Children's Aid Societies to work together more effectively for the sake of children whose lives they were affecting. June Maresca's passion for excellent process and her commitment to helping families are reflected in the materials used today to train new child protection mediators in Ontario.

Some ten years later, now a mediation trainer myself, I had a passionate and committed young student. A former child protection worker, Paul Brown stood out with his no-nonsense, direct, and sometimes unconventional approach. This was someone who knew what he wanted to accomplish as a family mediator.

The second edition of Guide to Child Protection Mediation stays true to the five key principles that informed Justice Maresca's work:

1. privileging the principle of party self-determination;
2. continuous awareness of the harm that can occur as a result of power imbalances;
3. knowledge of the powerful impacts of emotion and culture in family dispute resolution;
4. absolute respect for the craft of mediation;
5. and most importantly, keeping the children at the top of the triangle.

Well-written and well-organized, the 2nd edition of Guide to Child Protection Mediation is a valuable resource for child protection mediators new and experienced. Updated to reflect the changes in the 2018 Child, Youth and Family Services Act, this book explores all aspects of CP mediation within its legal, procedural and organizational contexts. Simply and clearly written, the Guide reflects the deep experience of someone who has conducted hundreds of child protection (and other family) mediations.

The Guide covers all the basics of contemporary CP med practice - from the governing legislation and policy directives, intake and screening, to the roles of all the players in this unique process. Paul provides practical guidance for CP mediators in working with the Office of the Children's Lawyer, family members, supporters and cheerleaders; on the use of technology; and on ensuring the voice and rights of the child are always at the forefront.

In plain language and illustrated with examples, Paul explains the legal requirements for confidentiality, respecting the unique rights of children who identify as First Nations, Inuit or Métis, and Openness in Adoption . Drawing on his own diverse experiences as a volunteer firefighter, martial artist, father and former child protection worker, Paul shares tips for self-care for professionals working in what can be a traumatizing role.

It is also full of gems such as:

- Tips for all mediators: "If a parent struggles to find a strength (about another party in the mediation) ask them for a strength from the child's perspective."
- Lists to help clients come to mediation with realistic expectations
- Strategies for empowering parties to be fully engaged participants in this challenging process
- a useful summary of the "don'ts" of CP med practice and
- handy appendices with precedents

Applying the five key principles listed above, the Guide challenges some conventions where, in Paul's experience, they are not well supported in principle or practice. Paul also does what all good mediators do – he demonstrates respect for different perspectives and honours the work of those who came before him.

The book is a thoughtful and practical contribution to what is still a new and evolving area of family dispute resolution practice in Ontario. I hope you enjoy it as much as I did.

Hilary Linton
J.D., LL.M., Acc. FM., FDRP Med.

PREFACE

In 2017, I published *A Guide To Child Protection Mediation in Ontario*. That was the first edition of this book, and one that came about due to frustration. One morning while laying in bed, I began thinking of some of the practices of other Child Protection Mediators in the communities where I worked. Although I embrace the idea of customizing the approach to best meet the needs of families, I am also passionate about staying true to the fundamental principles of the process. My frustration was, and remains, a result of mediators being focussed on their own wants and needs, and not honouring the true spirit of mediation; to help people work together and to level the playing field.

In my frustration, I thought "I'll show them. I'll write an article." Of course, the article would have then been posted on my website and in all honestly, very few people would have read it. Each week, I book Office Hours; a day when I am in the office reviewing files, writing reports, returning phone calls, and returning emails etc. Coincidentally, I had office hours booked that day and after getting my boys off to school, I started writing. After eight hours in front of my computer, I realized that I had way too much content for a simple article. It would need to be a book; this book.

Although I had written other books before, *Guide To CP Med* felt like the first "real" book I had written. My previous attempts at writing had either been chronicles of trips, or martial arts curriculums. Of course, writing and publishing a book was a learning process and within days of sending *Guide To CP Med* to print, I realized that I had missed lots of content.

Within two months of releasing the first edition, the second edition was already fifty pages longer. The book has been somewhat reorganized, some content dropped, and some areas have been expanded. Also, there have been changes at the Ministry level and in the legislation, and those need to be addressed in an effort to remain current.

I also learned that a title is important. Although *Guide To CP Med* is somewhat Ontario-centric in content, including "in Ontario" in the title limited my potential audience. I realized this while at the annual *Association for Family and Conciliation Courts* (AFCC) conference in Boston, MA. My book was on display for sale and even though there were over a thousand people in attendance, I sold very few copies. That's one of the reasons why in subsequent editions, "in Ontario" has been dropped from the title. Also, although the legislative content is geared towards Ontario, the rest of the content is useful for anyone practicing CP Med in any jurisdiction.

Thanks for reading, and I hope you find this information helpful...

Sincerely:

Paul Brown, HonBSc, AccFM, CP Med

ACKNOWLEDGEMENTS

Many people have helped with the progression of my mediation career, and with getting this book published. Some of them were sounding boards during the writing process, some helped edit the contents, and some helped keep me focused on the end goal. This book would not have been possible without the help of the following people.

First and foremost, I need to thank Nick Halmasy. Nick has been an incredible asset for me in my writing, and in discussing career ideas. He has reviewed and edited previous articles and books of mine, and also shared his perspectives from that of a Psychotherapist. I appreciate his insight, and his outlook. Our Irish Whiskey Strategic Planning Meetings are some of my favourite meetings to attend. Even though we sometimes get nothing accomplished, it's great to just bounce ideas off of one-another. Thank you, my friend. For more information about Nick, visit afterthecall.org.

Thank you, Carolyn McAlpine. It's great to have someone in my everyday life and practice that I can bounce ideas off, and with whom to discuss challenging cases. I always appreciate your input; even if your opinion is different than mine. And by different than mine, I mean wrong. haha. Thanks for always being direct, and holding me to task. For more information about Carolyn, visit kawarthacollaborative.com.

Hilary Linton of Riverdale Mediation in Toronto, Ontario, Canada. Even before my career officially began, you were very encouraging of my goals. You continue to invite me out to coach and lecture at your courses, and help build my mediation reputation. You have also shown endless encouragement with respect to my writing. You are an excellent resource, and a good friend. Thanks Hilary. For more information about Hilary, visit riverdalemediation.com

Laura Stevenson, it's great to have a friend "on the inside." Thanks for always being open to discussion about process, and how best to meet the needs of the Ministry, the agency, the facilitators and most importantly, families. I appreciate your willingness to listen, and your effort to help facilitate positive change. If only others "on the inside" had your vision...

Thank you, Carolyn Leach. You are the reason there are sections titled "*Narrative*" throughout this book. Your encouragement to share my experiences forced me to look more deeply at my writing, and at my mediation practice. You have also been great to work with, and an excellent resource when I have child-specific legislative uncertainties.

Thank you, Maryanne King. You continue to be a leader in the world of Openness Mediation. I truly appreciate your approachability, and willingness to help me find my rhythm in Openness Mediation. For more information on Maryanne, visit maryanneking.com.

My boys, Owen and Liam. You guys bring incredible joy to my life, and push me to be the best dad possible. Even during the toughest days, you continue to make me smile, laugh, and not take myself too seriously.

As always, my wife, Wendy. You have an incredibly patient spirit, and always encourage me to meet my goals; even when my goals sometimes take me away from home, husbanding, and parenting. You're the best! You are forever my rock, and help me find joy in each and every day. Thank you, and I love you, Babe.

MY STORY

My journey to becoming a mediator was anything but a direct path. The irony however is that as a young child, I always wanted to be a lawyer. Although I never became lawyer, I work hand-in-hand with them on an almost daily basis.

After high school, I studied Fitness and Lifestyle Management (FLM) at George Brown College in Toronto, Ontario Canada (In Canada, College refers to Community College and University is what most Americans refer to as College). When I graduated, I felt there was something missing. I had an excellent grasp on the physical body, but didn't know much about the mind. The FLM program dealt a lot with anatomy, physiology, injury prevention, and exercise prescription, but there was little focus on the psychological or emotional wellness of our future clients. So, I graduated from George Brown on a Friday in Spring 1998 and started my Psychology Degree at Trent University in Peterborough Ontario on the Monday.

Four years later, I had a life and career changing event. At 11:20am on July 22, 2002, I was involved in a motorcycle accident. Someone made a left turn in front of me, and I t-boned their vehicle. My bike stopped immediately, however I flew over the car. I landed head first on the pavement on the other side of the car, and slid down the road. As a result of the accident, I was off work for over two years.

During those two years, I accelerated my psychology studies. Prior to the accident, I was attending school part-time. After the accident, my days consisted of physiotherapy, massage therapy, and school. I also worked very hard at the gym to help with my physical rehabilitation.

Mediation is a mandatory step in the Accident Injury legal process in Ontario. For that process, I spent a day in Toronto with my lawyers, lawyers for the insurance companies, a lawyer from the city in which the accident happened, and a mediator. Early in the day, we broke into separate rooms and when all was said and done, I only saw the mediator three times the whole day. At the end of the day, I remember thinking that even though there was a settlement, the mediator did very little, yet was very expensive. I thought to myself, "That is a good job." Keep in mind, this was through the lens of someone in their twenties.

Around the same time, I received a continuing education brochure from Trent U. A certificate in mediation was one of the options, and I immediately signed up. There were two compulsory credits, and one elective credit necessary to receive the certificate. For my elective, I chose Family Mediation.

In Fall 2004, I went back to work, and in December of that year, I began working in Group Homes. One year later, I began working at Hastings Children's Aid Society (HCAS) in Belleville, Ontario. Also in December 2005, I graduated from Trent University with an Honours Bachelor of Science Degree in Psychology. I continued with my mediation studies while working at HCAS, because I knew my career wouldn't end there.

On November 30, 2006, another career-changing event; Bill 210 became law. Language was added to the Child and Family Services Act allowing for mediation as a means of working with families. Suddenly, my professional life came into focus. I would become a Child Protection Mediator...

As part of my journey, I also served for almost ten years as a volunteer, on-call firefighter in a rural community. Currently, I am an active member of *After The Call*, a Critical Incident Stress Management Team for First Responders. As a team, we assist emergency services with pre-incident planning, and debriefing after particularly challenging calls-for-service (eg death of a service member, fatal accidents, death of a child etc). These experiences have better equipped me to help families going through their own crises and trauma.

Today, my private practice is known for its specialty in Child Welfare Dispute Resolution but most importantly, my focus is on meeting the needs of families to create better outcomes; especially for children.

I'm sharing all of this because it demonstrates that you don't always need a straight line to reach your goals. In fact, sometimes the best outcomes come from diversity, struggle, and time. We often need to be reminded of this in order to better serve our families.

Disclaimer:

The opinions expressed herein are those of the author, and do not necessary reflect those of the Government of Ontario, the Ministry of Children & Youth Services, Ontario Association of Children's Aid Societies, or the Ontario Association for Family Mediation.

Table of Contents

FOREWORD iv
PREFACE vii
ACKNOWLEDGEMENTS ix
MY STORY xii
INTRODUCTION 1
TERMINOLOGY 2
DUTY TO REPORT 8
WHAT IS FAMILY MEDIATION? 14
WHAT IS CHILD PROTECTION MEDIATION? 26
   FUNDING 28
HOW TO BECOME A CHILD PROTECTION MEDIATOR 30
MINISTRY OF CHILDREN AND YOUTH SERVICES 32
WHAT IS THE CHILDREN'S AID SOCIETY 33
   CAS STRUCTURE 34
CHILD, YOUTH AND FAMILY SERVICES ACT 38
   ONTARIO RISK ASSESSMENT MODEL 41
   BILL 210 (Differential Response) 44
   ONTARIO REGULATION 496/ 06 45
   POLICY DIRECTIVE: CW 005-06 46
ELIGIBILITY SPECTRUM 49
CONSENT & CONFIDENTIALITY 52
   CHILDREN 12 AND OLDER 55
REFERRAL 57
   OFFICE OF THE CHILDREN'S LAWYER 58
SCREENING 60
   CONTACT RESTRICTIONS 66
LOCATION! LOCATION! LOCATION! 70
INTAKE 73
   SCHEDULING 73
   TECHNOLOGY 74
   CONFIDENTIALITY AGREEMENT 76
   FAMILY MEMBER 80
   WORKER 96

- SAFE TERMINATION 100
- VOICE OF THE CHILD 103
  - KATELYNN'S PRINCIPLE 103
  - CREATIVITY 108
  - OCL 109
- JOINT MEDIATION SESSION(S) 114
  - AGREEMENT TO MEDIATE 116
  - SHUTTLE MEDIATION 123
  - JOINT SESSION CONCLUSION 124
  - SUBSEQUENT JOINT MEDIATION SESSION(S) 126
- MEMORANDUM OF UNDERSTANDING 128
- FIRST NATIONS, INUIT, MÉTIS 130
- OPENNESS MEDIATION 135
  - LEGISLATION 137
  - REFERRAL 138
  - INTAKE 139
  - JOINT SESSION 144
- TOOL BOX 147
  - CULTURE FLOWER EXERCISE 148
  - COMMUNICATION-CONFLICT WAVE 152
  - FAMILY TRIANGLE EXERCISE 155
  - CHEERLEADERS 163
- SELF-CARE 166
- FUNCTIONAL DEFINITIONS OF MEDIATION 174
- WHAT *NOT* TO DO 175
- CONCLUSION 181
- ARTICLES 183
  - STICKS & STONES 184
  - FILLING THE VOID 187
  - THE FAMILY TRIANGLE 190
  - DEBRIEF & GRIEVE 194
- LETTERS 197
- THANK YOU 203
- APPENDIX 205
- REFERENCES 223

INTRODUCTION

Do you find yourself on autopilot sometimes when speaking with clients? Do you sometimes forget to share important elements of the mediation process with your clients, only to remember after they've left? How about the times when clients ask you specific questions about process or legislation, and you can't remember in the moment? It's happened to all of us.

This book is a concise review of the mediation process, and legislation including the recently proclaimed Child, Youth and Family Services Act (2017). Instead of having to reference multiple sources, and websites, it is a one-stop-shop for review. This book also includes useful tools to help you engage with your clients, streamline your appointments, and help clients move towards resolution. Although written with respect to Child Protection Mediation, the information contained herein is also useful in all areas of Family Mediation.

There are sections within several chapters titled "Narrative." In those sections, I share personal experiences. These may include positive experiences, but they may also include times when I made mistakes. Oftentimes, it is the mistakes from which we learn the most. My hope is that by sharing these experiences, you can avoid some of the same mistakes that I've made, and better serve your families.

Let's get started...

TERMINOLOGY

The following terms are used regularly in Child Protection Mediation, and are useful to know when facilitating this process. Terminology will be based on language of the Child Welfare system in the province of Ontario Canada.

Access - to visit with or be visited by a child

Child - any person under the age of eighteen (18).

Child In Need of Protection - a designation given to a child who MAY be at risk of physical and/ or emotional harm. In the legal system, only a judge may make an finding that a child is in need of protection under the Child, Youth and Family Services Act (CYFSA). This finding is necessary before a judge may make an order under the CYFSA.

Child Protection Worker - a Director, a local director or a person who meets the prescribed requirements and who is authorized by a Director or local director for the purposes of commencing child protection proceedings and for other prescribed purposes.

Children's Aid Society (CAS) or "Society" - an approved agency designated by the Minister of Children and Youth Services for a specified territorial jurisdiction, and for any or all of the functions of a society set out in subsection 35(1) of the Child, Youth & Family Services Act (CYFSA).

Closed Mediation - Neither parties nor the mediator may give evidence in a legal proceeding about what was said during the process. Only the terms of any settlement may be disclosed.

Child Protection Mediation is a Closed Mediation.

Court - Ontario Court of Justice (OCJ) or the Family Branch of the Superior Court of Justice (SCJ). The CYFSA is provincial legislation and as such, it is heard in the Ontario Court of Justice. In communities where there is only an SCJ, CYFSA matters are heard in the Family Branch of the SCJ.

Custody - the legal right to make important decisions about the child's care, education, religious instruction, and their general welfare.

> *Joint Custody* - a shared right to make important decisions about the child regardless of the parenting schedule. The parties work cooperatively to make important decisions together.
>
> *Sole Custody* - one person has the exclusive right to make important decisions about the child regardless of the parenting schedule. The person does not have an obligation to consult with the other party prior to making the decision.
>
> *Shared Custody* - when the child spends more than forty percent (40%) of the time over the course of a year with each parent. This term does NOT relate to decision-making (i.e. "Custody"), however it may have an impact on Child Support.

Split Custody - where each parent has custody of one of more children (ie there are multiple children from the relationship, however all of the children do not live with the same parent).

Eligibility Spectrum - a tool designed to assist CAS staff in making consistent and accurate decisions about eligibility for service at the time of referral. The Eligibility Spectrum was most recently revised in 2016.

Extended Society Care (formerly Crown Wardship) - the Crown (ie the State) has the rights and responsibilities of a parent for the purpose of the child's care, custody and control, and the Crown's powers, duties and obligations in respect of the child, except those assigned to a Director by the CYFSA or the regulations, shall be exercised and performed by the Society caring for the child. An order that the child be found in need of protection is required before an order of Extended Society Care is made.

Interim Society Care (formerly Society Wardship) - when a child is placed in the care and custody of the Society by way of a court order for a specified period not exceeding twelve months. An order that the child be found in need of protection is required before an order of Interim Society Care is made. The Society has the rights and responsibilities of a parent for the purpose of the child's care, custody and control.

Kinship - a family member or close friend of the family. Typically used in reference to a placement outside of the family home, but not in foster care or group care.

Open Mediation - Parties and the mediator may give evidence in a legal proceeding about what happened during the process, including evidence about what offers were made.

Parent - can be a biological parent, adoptive parent, or someone who has lawful custody of the child, or an individual who has demonstrated an intention to treat the child as part of their family, or has acknowledged parentage of the child and provided for the child's support.

Place of Safety - a foster home, a hospital, a person's home that satisfies the requirements of subsection CYFSA s.74(4) or a place or one of a class of places designated as a place of safety by a Director or local director under CYFSA s.39, but does not include a place of temporary detention, of open custody or of secure custody.

Section 74(4) of the CYFSA indicates a person's home is a place of safety for a child if:
 a) the person is a relative of the child or a member of the child's extended family or community; and
 b) a society or, in the case of a First Nations, Inuk or Métis child, a society or a child and family services authority, has conducted an assessment of the person's home in accordance with the prescribed procedures and is satisfied that the person is willing and able to provide a safe home environment for the child.

Plan of Care - a plan designed to meet a child's particular needs while in the care of the Society. It shall be prepared within thirty (30) days of the child's or young person's admission to the residential placement. The child has a right to participate in the development of their individual plan of care, and in any changes made to it.

Plan of Service - Used when the family is working voluntarily (ie not in court) with the CAS. A plan outlining how the CAS and family with work together for a specified period of time. It outlines tasks required of the CAS and family members.

Primary Residence - the residence in which a child lives the majority of the time. This often has financial implications related to Child Support, and income tax credits.

Protection Application - a court application filed by CAS when the Society believes a child needs protection because of harm, or believes that a child is at risk of suffering harm. This is typically filed if the family is not willing to work with CAS voluntarily.

Referral - when someone contacts the local CAS to report concerns with respect to the well being of a child.

Regulation - a rule or directive made and maintained by an authority designed to control or govern conduct. Compliance with regulations is mandatory.

Standards - policies developed by the Ministry of Children and Youth Services as a means of directing and measuring specific program areas. Standards are mandatory, and establish a minimum level of performance to meet compliance requirements.

Supervision Order - when a child is placed in the care and custody of a parent or another person, subject to the supervision of the society, for a specified period of at least three months and not more than twelve months. An order that the child be found in need of protection is required before a Supervision Order is made.

Statute - provides overall direction and legal requirements that describe the official mandate and parameters of service delivery. For CAS, the key statute is the CYFSA.

United Nations Convention on the Rights of the Child - a human rights treaty involving 196 countries, including Canada (1990) and the United States of America (1995). The convention sets out civil, political, economic, social, health, and cultural rights of children. The convention defines a child as "any human being under the age of eighteen (18), unless the age of majority is attained earlier under national legislation."

DUTY TO REPORT

Although the Child, Youth and Family Services Act (CYFSA) will be covered in further detail later in this book, Section 125 of the CYFSA requires special attention. Section 125 of the CYFSA is with respect to *Duty To Report*. Duty To Report relates to everyone; not just those involved in Child Protection Mediation.

Duty To Report is a person's responsibility to notify the local CAS if they believe a child is at risk of neglect or harm. The CYFSA says "if a person, including a person who performs professional or official duties with respect to children..." The CYFSA then goes a step further, and lists specific professionals. In fact, Section 125(6)(d) specifically references mediators as having a duty to report if they have reasonable belief that a child is at risk of harm. Although the CYFSA highlights professionals as having a responsibility, they are included in the larger group of citizens. As such, every person (with the exception of solicitor-client privilege) has an obligation to report if they honestly believe a child is at risk of harm.

This section of the CYFSA supersedes any other act. That is to say that there is no legal reason that a person can refuse to report if they believe a child is in need of protection. If a service provider who provides services with respect to children knowingly does not report concerns that a child may be in need of protection, they may be charged. If convicted, they face the possibility of a fine of up to five thousand dollars ($5000).

If a person believes that a child may be in need of protection, it is that person's responsibility to provide the local CAS with the information. The person receiving the information first-hand must make the referral; not someone else within their agency. For example, if a teacher receives information that a child may be at risk of harm, it is the teacher who must make the referral; not the school principal.

Reasons to make a referral, and why CAS may become involved with a family include but are not limited to:
- physical harm or risk of physical harm inflicted by a caregiver or as a result of lack of supervision or neglect
- sexual assault/ exploitation (including child pornography) or risk of sexual assault/ exploitation (including child pornography) by a caregiver or by someone else and the caregiver fails to protect the child
- failure to provide for the child's medical needs
- emotional harm demonstrated by serious anxiety, depression, withdrawal, self-destructive/ aggressive behaviour or delayed development, and there are reasonable grounds to believe the emotional harm is a result of actions or failure to act by the caregiver.
- emotional harm or risk of emotional harm noted above and the caregiver does not provide or consent to services to alleviate the harm.
- the child suffers from a mental, emotional or developmental condition that if not remedied, could seriously impair their development and the caregiver does not provide or does not/ cannot consent to treatment to alleviate the condition.
- child has been abandoned either by choice or by caregiver death
- child is younger than twelve, and has killed or seriously injured a person or caused serious damage to another person's property, AND the caregiver refuses or is unable to consent to treatment services.
- child is younger than twelve and on more than one occasion injured another person or caused damage to another person's property with the encouragement of the caregiver or due to lack of supervision.

When making a referral to CAS, some people fear retaliation. From a legal perspective, there will be no action against a person who makes a referral to CAS in good faith. Also, employers are not permitted to discipline staff in any way for having made a referral to CAS. The Act also allows for the protection of a referents identity. The identity of the referent cannot be released to the identified family or to the person believed to have caused the child to be in need of protection unless required or permitted in a court proceeding.

If you are uncertain as to whether or not information received meets the threshold for child welfare intervention, call the local child welfare agency. You can provide the agency with the information without disclosing the names of the parties. Inform the agency that you are calling as you are uncertain if the information received meets the necessary threshold for service. If the agency representative informs you that the information does meet the threshold, you should then provide the agency with the names of the parties involved. If the information does not meet the threshold, then disclosure of the names is not necessary.

Depending on the nature of the referral, it may or may not be beneficial to inform the parties that you have notified the child welfare agency of the information. Generally speaking, it is best to be transparent, and inform the party that you need to report the information. However, if there is a concern that a child may be harmed as a result of informing the party, then the party should not be told of the child welfare referral.

In 2017, the Child, Youth and Family Services Act (CYFSA) was proclaimed. The most significant change to the legislation was that sixteen (16) and seventeen (17) year olds would be recognized as being eligible for protection services. In spite of that, there is not a legislative requirement to report concerns with respect to sixteen (16) and seventeen (17) years old. That is to say that there is no official Duty To Report for them. That said, Section 125(4) states that an individual *may* make a report if they have concerns.

FAMILY
MEDIATION

WHAT IS FAMILY MEDIATION?

Mediation is a form of Alternative Dispute Resolution (ADR), and ADR processes are typically considered as an alternative to litigation (going to court). Other forms of ADR include but are not limited to:
- Arbitration
- Collaborative Law
- Family Group Conferencing/ Decision-Making
- Mediation-Arbitration
- Restorative Justice

Mediation is a process of negotiation in relationships that is intended to resolve differences with the use of a neutral, specially-trained facilitator. The purpose of mediation is to level the playing field in an effort to assist the parties in resolving their issues in a constructive, and supportive manner.

Participants in mediation are encouraged to actively participate in the process, while the mediator helps them to focus on their needs (both individual and as a group), and interests. By being involved in finding solutions, the parties are more inclined to honour the agreement that they reach. This creates greater compliance after the fact.

Success in mediation lies partly in the skills of the mediator, but also with the readiness of the parties. Regardless of how skilled the mediator is or how empathetic they are to the situation, there is little the mediator can do to facilitate an effective process if the clients are not ready to move forward. The true success in mediation lies with the clients. Mediators need to remember this, and also remind the parties of their (the party's) success at the end of a successful mediation.

THE MEDIATOR IS ONLY AS EFFECTIVE AS THE PEOPLE IN THE ROOM

Family Mediation is a voluntary process. Any of the parties may withdraw from the process at any time, and it should not be used against them. The mediator may also withdraw from the process if they believe continuing the process may create an unsafe environment either emotionally, physically, or in the family's legal situation. The mediator may also stop the process if they do not believe the parties are making progress. There is no point in continuing the process and wasting time and money if there is no forward movement. At times, the mediator and the parties have a different perception of what constitutes forward movement in a mediation.

More often than not, parties to a Family Mediation involve parents going through a separation or divorce. In reality however, Family Mediation skills and strategies may be used to help extended family members resolves various differences as well. Some examples of topics covered in Family Mediation include but are not limited to:
- Custody and access to children
- Financial settlement after a separation
- communication strategies among parents or other family members
- parenting strategies
- schedules related to use of joint family properties
- family estate division
- elder mediation

In Family Mediation, the mediator must have a confidential, intake appointment with each of the parties. During that appointment, the mediator is screening for client readiness, family violence, abuse, power imbalances, mental health concerns, substance use concerns and more. After meeting with each client privately, the mediator then makes a decision as to whether or not the mediation will move forward to the joint mediation session. During the joint mediation session, parties may either be in the same room or different rooms. Much of this information will be covered in more detail in future chapters, as there is considerable process overlap among Family Mediation and Child Protection Mediation.

The primary focus of the mediator is to manage the process in order to provide a safe environment for the parties, and a structure that leads them towards opportunities for resolution. The mediator's role also includes "reality checks," so that the parties are able to reach a sustainable solution to the issues being discussed.

MEDIATORS ARE AGENTS OF REALITY

Below is a list of reasons why mediation may be effective:
- less costly than going to court
- faster than going to court
- the clients control the process
- improves relationships
- less stressful than going to court

FINANCIAL FAMILY MEDIATION

Financial Family Mediation (FFM) typically involves settling financial issues during a separation or divorce, and may include discussions about property and possessions. Financial mediation is a very complex process, but with different complexities than other family mediations. Not only are you dealing with the emotions of the separation or divorce, the mediator is also dealing with the emotions related to a person's financial relationship. Further, there are very complicated laws to be aware of when negotiating financial settlements.

A very simplistic way of approaching FFM's is to list assets and liabilities, and split the difference. Unfortunately, this does not create a true picture of the financial dynamics, because the division of certain assets and debts may have diverse tax implications. Without knowing those tax implications, the parties may not be aware of the full impact of their decisions. There are also complex financial situations involving investments and pensions.

It is highly recommended that FFM's only be completed by a lawyer-mediator or someone with significant training specific to the laws in this area. Another option is to ensure that the parties have consulted with lawyers, and provided complete financial disclosure. Without the necessary training however, a mediator should not attempt an FFM without lawyers present for the joint mediation session. As with any type of mediation, the mediator should not work outside of their scope of training.

COURT-CONNECTED FAMILY MEDIATION

In Ontario, there is a court-connected family mediation program funded by the Ministry of the Attorney General (MAG). This program consists of On-Site Mediation, Off-Site Mediation, and Information and Referral Coordinators. The court-connected mediation service providers are also responsible for providing the Mandatory Information Program (MIP) in their community.

Approximately every three to five years, MAG puts out a Request For Proposal (RFP) to provide court-connected family mediation services in Ontario. Each RFP is for a specific geographical area, but the nature of the services are similar across the province. Each service provider must provide a list of accredited mediators (or equivalent) on their roster, as well as individuals available to provide information related to family law resources in the community.

Information about the Court-Connected Mediation service providers in various communities can be found on the MAG website.

Mandatory Information Program (MIP)

Mandatory Information Programs (MIP's) are available in family court locations across Ontario and depending on the location, the program may be available in French as well as English. MIP's are free to attend but as the name suggests, they are mandatory once a family court case has been initiated. Individuals may also contact the local service provider to attend MIP's on a voluntary basis (ie even if they are not involved in court).

Once a family court case has been initiated, both parties are required to attend for an information session. Some exceptions to attendance at a MIP are:
- previous attendance at a MIP (ie for another matter)
- parties are requesting a ruling on consent (ie both parties agree to the order being requested)
- only claims are for divorce, costs, or an order incorporating the terms of an agreement or prior court order

Generally speaking, MIP's are facilitated by a lawyer and a mental health professional. In many communities, mediator's are considered the mental health professional. MIP's are designed to provide attendees with information about separation and divorce and the legal process, including:
- effects of separation and divorce on children and adults
- alternatives to litigation

- family law issues
- family court process
- local resources and programs for families going through separation or divorce

MIP's are scripted, and presenters are encouraged to "stick to the script." This is so there is a standard level of information being delivered across the province. In principle, an individual attending a MIP in Ottawa, Ontario should receive the same program information as an individual attending a MIP in Toronto. One the MIP is completed, presenters generally stay to answer questions. There are also brochures and pamphlets available for attendees.

On-Site Mediation

On-Site Mediation refers to mediations that occur at the courthouse. The On-Site mediator is typically located in the Family Law Information Centre (FLIC) within the courthouse. In order to participate in an On-Site mediation, the parties are supposed to be on the family court docket on that date. Mediators are not supposed to schedule On-Site mediations in advance of that date, however this does happen in some jurisdictions.

On-Site mediation is a free service, and it is designed to help expedite the court process on that day. The process involves a brief, confidential intake appointment with each party, and then a joint mediation session if the case is appropriate for mediation. If the parties reach an agreement, the agreement may be presented to the judge in hopes of it being made into a court order. Discussions at On-Site mediations are also generally limited to topics such as custody, access, and child support. In total, an On-Site mediation process should take two hours or less. If the mediation is going to take longer or the topics for discussion are more comprehensive, the case may be referred to an Off-Site mediation.

All On-Site mediations are closed mediations.

Off-Site Mediation

Off-Site Mediation refers to mediations that occur away from the courthouse; typically at the mediator's office. Although facilitated by the court-connected service provider, families do not have to be involved in the court process to take advantage of the Off-Site mediation programs.

Also in contrast to On-Site mediation, Off-Site mediation is fee-for-service; not free. Although both parties receive a free, comprehensive intake appointment, each party will pay a fee if the matter proceeds to a joint mediation session. Fees are on a sliding scale, and the program is unique in that each party pays according to their own income. Fees for each party can range from five dollars per hour up to one hundred and fifty dollars per hour. Although this makes mediation more accessible to some people, the difference in fees can sometimes create resentment amongst the parties.

With Off-Site mediations, each party meets with the mediator for a free, confidential intake appointment. Once the intake appointments are completed, the mediator will make a decision if the mediation moves forward or not. If the mediation does move forward, the parties then pay for their portion of the fees based on the agreed upon sliding scale. In some communities, fees are paid at the end of each appointment and in other communities, service providers ask the clients to pay a six-hour retainer up front.

Because Off-Site mediations are not under the same time constraints as On-Site mediations, the topics of discussion are often more complex. Among those topics may be financial issues. In some communities, only lawyers are used to mediate financial issues. In other communities, clinical mediators do comprehensive mediations that include financial issues.

Another contrast to On-Site mediation is that parties choose whether or not they would prefer a closed mediation or an open mediation. MAG's definition of open mediation however, is not the true definition of open mediation. The MAG definition of open mediation is that the mediator may list any unresolved issues, however the mediation remains without prejudice and confidential. A true open mediation is neither without prejudice nor confidential, and the mediators and the parties may be called to give evidence about what happened during the mediation.

Information and Referral Coordinator

Also located in the FLIC is the Information and Referral Coordinator (IRC). An IRC is generally at court on the days when family court is in session. The role of the IRC is to provide information about resources available in the community to assist families. They are to provide information only; not advice. This is especially important in the context of family law matters. The IRC service is also free to use.

Due to funding models and scheduling demands, it is not uncommon for the On-Site mediator and the IRC to be one and the same.

HOW TO BECOME A FAMILY MEDIATOR

In Ontario, mediation is not regulated. As a result, anybody can call themselves a mediator. An individual may have no experience dealing with families, no knowledge of screening for power imbalances, and no skills to design a safe meeting environment. Yet, they may still call themselves a Family Mediator. Thankfully, the public is becoming more educated as to the benefits of working with a trained mediator, so the incidents of unskilled mediators remaining active is decreasing. Also, the public is more often seeking out individuals that belong to a professional organization, as there is an expected standard of practice.

There are several organizations in Ontario offering certification as a family mediator. They include, but are not limited to:
- Alternative Dispute Resolution Institute of Ontario (ADRIO)
- Family Dispute Resolution Institute of Ontario (FDRIO)
- Family Mediation Canada (FMC)
- Ontario Association for Family Mediation (OAFM)

Although there are differences between the organizations for certification, there are many similarities. Some of the similarities include:
- professional liability insurance
- a university degree
- introduction to conflict resolution training
- family mediation training
- training in screening for domestic violence and power imbalances
- an internship including cases mediated to agreement

In addition to the above criteria, some organizations also require a written exam, a video-taped role-play assessment, and a skills assessment to become certified. Of particular interest however is that not all of the organizations require family law training for non-family lawyers. This is changing, however there remain many mediators in the field without any knowledge of family law. This is a significant concern as these mediators are often providing legal information as part of their mediation process.

CHILD PROTECTION MEDIATION

WHAT IS CHILD PROTECTION MEDIATION?

In Ontario, the prescribed methods of Child Welfare ADR include Child Protection Mediation, Family Group Conferencing (also referred to as Family Group Decision-Making in Ontario), and various First Nations processes. There are other forms of ADR that have been approved by the Ministry of Children and Youth Services (MCYS), however those methods are used on a smaller scale in individual communities. For the purposes of this text, the term ADR will refer exclusively to Child Protection Mediation, Family Group Conferencing/ Family Group Decision-Making, and approved First Nations methods.

Child Protection Mediation (CP Med) is a specialized form of Family Mediation, and follows many of the same principles. It is a voluntary process involving family members, a representative from CAS, and sometimes a lawyer appointed by the Office of the Children's Lawyer. It is a process wherein a family, CAS worker, and when assigned, a lawyer for the child work together to plan for the well-being of the child. It is facilitated by a specially trained, impartial facilitator who has no decision making authority. The overarching purpose of CP Med is to help the parties come to an agreement that addresses the identified child protection concerns.

CP Med is emotional work. The families involved may have had their children removed from their care, or may be facing that possibility if their situation does not change. They may be involved in a complex legal battle with CAS, and have an overwhelming sense of powerlessness. Many of the clients involved in the child welfare system are underprivileged, feel marginalized, and often feel unheard. For these reasons, it is incredibly important that the facilitator be well-versed in mediation strategies, and have an open mind for the population with whom they work.

The purpose of CP Med is not to determine if a child is in need of protection. When CAS opens a file, they do so because they believe that there is a child in need of protection. From a legal perspective, only a judge may make a "finding" that a child is need of protection. A "finding" must be in place prior to a judge making an order in Child Welfare court.

Child Welfare ADR was added to Child Welfare legislation to assist families and CAS with working through a plethora of issues. CP Med is only one method available, and may be used to explore solutions to almost any issue in a child protection case. The intent was to help families and CAS work more cooperatively. Unfortunately, most CAS agencies have come to view CP Med as a means to assist only families engaged in custody and access disputes. Although not traditional child protection cases, these files can often have levels of conflict that quickly put the child at risk of harm. As a result, CAS intervenes and often makes a referral to CP Med.

Recently, a shift has started to take place wherein CAS is also making referrals for other types of cases. Although not an exhaustive list, some examples of possible CP Med referrals include:

- Custody and Access
- Customary Care Arrangements
- Family Communication
- Terms of CAS Involvement/ Plan of Service Tasks
- File transfer from another agency
- Adoption Openness
- Parent-Teen Conflict
- Reintegration Strategies

FUNDING

The ADR process is funded by MCYS, and funneled to facilitators by a Transfer Payment Agency (TPA). MCYS also funds the CAS agencies in the province, however the facilitators are not paid by the CAS. Most facilitators in the province are private clinicians. In an effort to remain neutral and transparent, mediators should ensure that clients are aware that the funding for CP Med and CAS comes from the same Ministry, however the mediator is not paid by CAS. I often draw a diagram similar to that in *Figure 1* to illustrate this point.

Figure 1: Funding Model

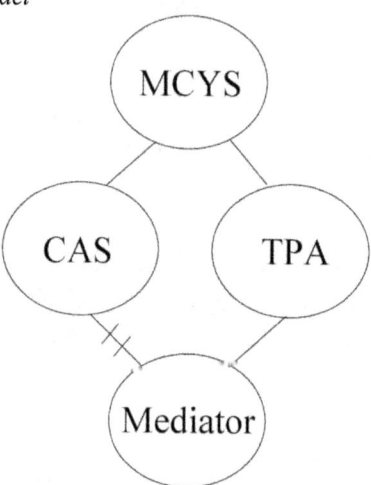

Of note, most TPA's have held their contract as such since shortly after Bill 210 was implemented in 2006. That is to say that there has not been a Request For Proposal (RFP) since the inception of Child Welfare ADR in Ontario. This is concerning as there are considerable differences among TPA's across the province. Further, there may not be incentive for TPA's to remain current on trends in the industry.

There does not appear to be much oversight from the Ministry with respect to program implementation, and some TPA's have made process changes that do not fall in line with the philosophies of CP Med. One example of this would be directing mediators to have CAS supervisors present during joint mediation sessions (more about this later). Rarely are mediators or families consulted prior to these changes being implemented, and this further drives a wedge between families and CAS. It also reinforces the perceived power imbalances in CP Med. It is imperative that trained CP Mediators push back on this, and ensure that the philosophy of mediation is respected and adhered to.

As mentioned in the Family Mediation section, the Ministry of the Attorney General (MAG) has a court-connected mediation in the province. When an agency is awarded a contract to provide the court-connected mediation in a community, the contract is time limited. Typically, the contract is for three years with an option to extend at the end. When the contract expires, organizations must then submit an updated RFP, and there are no guarantees that the existing contract holder will remain as the service provider in that community. Although putting together an RFP is daunting, it serves a purpose. MAG is able to monitor the various programs closely, and it forces organizations to ensure they are providing the best service possible to their clients.

It would likely be beneficial to the clients we service if MCYS would put out an RFP with respect to CP Med.

HOW TO BECOME A CHILD PROTECTION MEDIATOR

In order to do CP Med work in the province of Ontario, mediators must be on the Ontario Child Protection Mediation Roster. The roster is currently managed by Ontario Association for Family Mediation (OAFM) on behalf of MCYS. Interested mediators must complete a five day course in order to be listed on the roster. To register for the course, candidates must meet the following criteria:

1. Accreditation as a Family Mediator (OAFM), Certification as a Family Mediator (FMC), or Chartered status as a Family Mediator (ADRIO), or equivalency, defined as:
   a) A professional degree or diploma in the social services or children's services;
   b) Completion of at least 60 hours of training in Family Mediation, to include 20 hours of skill based training;
   c) Completion of 14 hours of domestic violence training; and
   d) Completion of at least 10 family law mediation cases to the point of agreement, with submission of Memorandum of Understanding.

2. Proof of professional liability insurance.

3. A satisfactory criminal record check or submission of your security clearance number, both obtained within the last three years.

4. Three satisfactory professional references, two of which must be from people with whom you have co-mediated a family matter or who have referred family law cases to you.

5. Signed declaration form to abide by the OAFM CP Med Code of Professional Conduct.

6. A current curriculum vitae.

The five day CP Med course is an evaluated course. Participants must successfully pass a written test as well as evaluated role play exercises. Upon successful completion, candidates will be added to the Ontario Provincial Mediation Roster. Once a mediator is on the provincial roster, they may then attempt to have their name added to sub-rosters held by the local TPA's. CP Mediators should be aware that being accepted on the provincial roster neither guarantees acceptance on a TPA's sub-roster, nor does it guarantee cases will be assigned.

Unfortunately, at this time, there is no obligation to complete an internship specific to CP Med. Many of the mediators practicing CP Med at this time have little-to-no experience in child welfare prior to becoming a CP Mediator. The lack of internship requirements sets these individuals up for failure, because child welfare is an incredibly dynamic field of practice.

Currently, there is no requirement for CP Mediators to have ongoing training specific to CP Med. This is concerning. Although they are required to maintain their membership with their Family Mediation professional organization, for some, this requires only ten hours of continuing education.

Finally, the legal piece. Prior to July 1, 2016, OAFM did not require non family lawyers to have Family Law training to become accredited. People accredited before July 1, 2016 remain eligible to take the CP Med training which means that there are CP Mediators practicing today that have not been trained in Family Law. As part of continuing education requirements, best practice is that CP Mediators remain current on legislation relating to Family Law and Child Welfare. They should also remain current on the service delivery models being utilized by various CAS agencies.

MINISTRY OF CHILDREN AND YOUTH SERVICES

In 2003, the Ministry of Children and Youth Services (MCYS) was created to coordinate services for families and children. The Ministry's overarching goals are to:
- make it easier for families to find the services they need to give children the best start in life
- make it easier for families to access the services they need at all stages of a child's development
- help youth to become productive adults

MCYS administers the CYFSA with the exception of sections related specifically to adoption records.

WHAT IS THE CHILDREN'S AID SOCIETY

The Children's Aid Society (CAS) is a "non-government organization." Although they are funded by MCYS, they are independent from the government of Ontario. CAS is dedicated to ensuring the protection and well-being of children in the province. In the United States, a comparable term is Child Protective Services.

Currently (2018), there are forty-four CAS agencies, and four First Nations CAS agencies in Ontario. In recent years, there have been amalgamations to decrease the number of CAS agencies in the province, and it is generally understood that there will be more amalgamations to further reduce that number. All of these agencies belong to a larger organization known as the Ontario Association of Children's Aid Societies (OACAS). OACAS has been around since 1920, and is responsible for advocacy, government relations, public education, and training. OACAS is governed by a voluntary Board of Directors.

Section 35(1) of the CYFSA describes the functions of CAS as:

a) investigate allegations or evidence that children may be in need of protection;
b) protect children where necessary;
c) provide guidance, counselling and other services to families for protecting children or for the prevention of circumstances requiring the protection of children;
d) provide care for children assigned or committed to its care under this Act;
e) supervise children assigned to its supervision under this Act;
f) place children for adoption under Part VIII (Adoption and Adoption Licensing); and

g) perform any other duties given to it by this Act or the regulations or any other Act.

CAS STRUCTURE

The hierarchy of CAS starts with front-line workers. Front-line workers report to supervisors, who report to managers. Managers report to the Director(s) of Service, who then reports to the Executive Director. The Executive Director is primarily a political position, and they report to a volunteer Board of Directors and MCYS.

Figure 2: CAS Structure

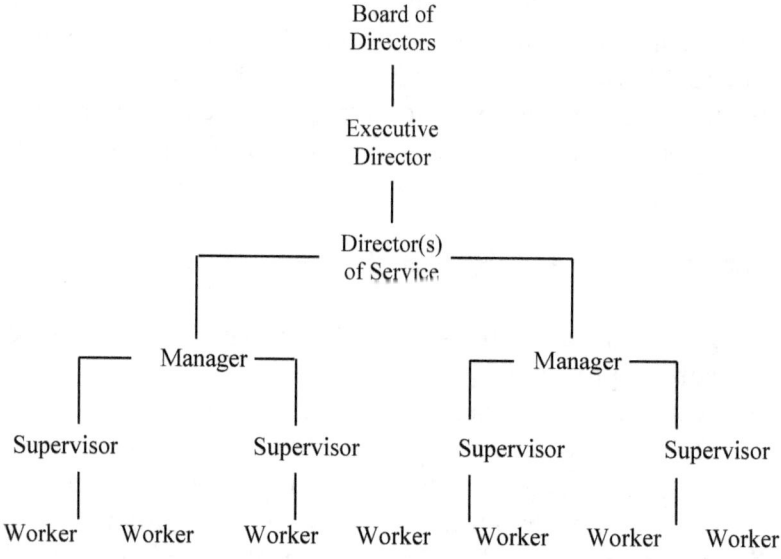

In CP Med, mediators primarily deal with front-line workers and sometimes, supervisors. Front-line workers include but are not limited to Child Protection Workers (often referred to as Family

Services Workers or simply "Workers"), Children's Services Workers, Adoption Workers and sometimes, Resource Workers. In some agencies, Family Services Workers are divided into Intake Workers (handle the investigations), and Ongoing Workers (work with the family long-term). In other agencies, they are occasionally referred to as Generic Workers as they manage both Intake and Ongoing cases. Family Services Workers are the case managers of the protection file.

Children's Services Workers work with children who have been admitted to CAS care. This may include children who are in Interim Society Care or Extended Society Care. Children's Services Workers are just that; the worker for the child.

An Adoption Worker is responsible for facilitating the adoption process for both the family that is adopting, and the child who is being adopted. Adoption workers often use mediation to discuss openness with respect to children and birth families. This is essential in our technologically modern world, as there is a high probability that adoptive children will use technology to seek out their birth family later in life. It is better to discuss some planning for that well in advance.

Resource Workers are responsible for finding placements for children who are admitted to CAS care. They are also responsible for assessing potential foster placements, and kinship homes. Kinship placements are often used as an alternative to admitting a child into CAS care. The goal of kinship placements is to better support family relationships. It is also generally more cost effective for CAS to support in-family placements than it is to admit a child into CAS care.

Most kinship placements are voluntary, and do not require court intervention. For a child to be admitted to CAS care by way of an apprehension (non-voluntary placement), the matter must be heard in court. If a child is apprehended, CAS must bring the matter to court within five days of the child being admitted to CAS care. In the event of a Temporary Care Agreement between the parents and the CAS placing the child in CAS care voluntarily, then court is not necessary.

At this time, Child Protection Workers are neither required to be Social Workers, nor do they have to be registered with the *Ontario College of Social Workers and Social Service Workers*. Child Protection Workers are tasked with doing Child Protection work; not social work. They often have varied degrees and education such as Psychology, Criminology, Sociology etc. Although workers previously had to complete New Worker Training to become authorized, the authorization varied across the province.

In 2017, the authorization process became uniform across the province of Ontario based on recommendations from the Coroner's Inquest into the death of Katelynn Sampson (more on this in the *Voice of the Child* chapter). Now, new workers (non-authorized workers) must complete one hundred and twenty (120) hours of training both online and in person. Within the new curriculum, there are eight courses which the non-authorized worker must complete. The courses include:
1. Cornerstones of Child Welfare (ie History)
2. Legal Framework of Child Welfare
3. Maltreatment and Child Development
4. Intake and Investigation
5. Professional Resiliency and Self-Care
6. Legal Process and Court Procedures
7. Ongoing Services, Part 1
8. Ongoing Services, Part 2

Non-authorized workers will be required to pass each course prior to moving on to the next course. Once all of the course work is completed, the non-authorized worker is required to complete the

Authorization Candidacy Exam (ACE). Once successful in passing the ACE, workers will be eligible for authorization. The requirements are to be completed within six months of being hired.

Individuals are given two opportunities to pass the ACE. If they are unsuccessful, it is recommended that the individual not be authorized. It should be noted however that it is the Director of each Child Welfare agency who authorizes the workers; not the MCYS. So, even though a person is unsuccessful on the ACE, an agency Director may still choose to authorize that person.

CHILD, YOUTH AND FAMILY SERVICES ACT

As mentioned earlier, CP Med has its roots in Family Mediation. Fortunately in recent years, a formal education in Family Law has become mandatory for Family Mediators to receive their certification. Although not extensive, Family Mediators need to understand how the laws are applied to families in order to provide families with an effective process. CP Mediators should have a strong working knowledge of the Family Law Act, Children's Law Reform Act, and Divorce Act, as there is often an overlap in CP matters and family court matters.

In Ontario, the Child, Youth and Family Services Act (CYFSA) is the legislation that governs all Children's Aid Societies in the province. They are the rules under which the CAS operates. When I meet with clients, I describe the CYFSA as the rules of the CAS; much like the Highway Traffic Act contains the rules of the roads. Provisions of the CYFSA relating to the age of protection came into force on January 1, 2018. As of the publication of this book however, not all other sections had been proclaimed. The predecessor to the CYFSA was the Child and Family Services Act (CFSA). In the CFSA, the age of eligibility for protection services was limited to under sixteen (16). Under the CYFSA however, the eligibility for protection services has increased to those under eighteen (18) years of age. For those aged sixteen (16) and seventeen (17), their participation in services is completely voluntary.

The main purpose of the CYFSA is to "promote the best interests, protection and well-being of children." It emphasizes that CAS interventions should be from least intrusive to most intrusive and ideally, on mutual consent of the family and CAS. The Act also stresses that services to families should be respectful of the family's cultural, religious, and regional differences.

To be an effective CP Mediator, you need to have a strong working knowledge of Child Welfare Legislation in your Province or State. Each region has different rules and responsibilities and without having a knowledge of the legalities, mediators may be working outside of their safety net. This may in turn set them up for legal consequences. An example of this is with respect to definitions.

Section 2(1) of the CYFSA defines a Service Provider as:

the Minister, a licensee, a person or entity, including a society, that provides a service funded under this act, or a prescribed person or entity.

Included in the definition of Service, also in Section 2(1) of the CYFSA is "a prescribed service."

Considering ADR is a "prescribed service," funded by the MCYS, the CP Mediator is a "Service Provider" as defined by the CYFSA. As a result, the CP Mediator is bound by all parts of the Act relating to being a Service Provider. This carries significant responsibilities, and it is in the mediator's best interest to understand their role.

The section of the CYFSA that directly relates to ADR is Section 17(1). Section 17(1) states:

If a child is or may be in need of protection under this Act, a society shall consider whether a prescribed method of alternative dispute resolution could assist in resolving any issue related to the child or a plan for the child's care.

This is important as it implies that in every file that is open to CAS for protection services, CAS <u>must</u> consider ADR. To be clear, the Act does not say that ADR must occur with every file, but ADR must be considered. If a file closes without ADR being considered, CAS has not met their criteria as set out in the legislation.

Section 17(2) states:

If the issue referred to in subsection (1) relates to a First Nations, Inuk or Métis child, the society shall consult with a representative chosen by each of the child's Bands and First Nations, Inuit or Métis communities to determine whether an alternative dispute resolution process established by the Bands and communities or another prescribed alternative dispute resolution process could assist in resolving the issue.

*Note: Inuk is singular for Inuit

With respect to children who are First Nations, Inuit or Métis, they are entitled to receive services that include their specific traditions. The Act highlights that the child's Band or First Nations community will be contacted, to enquire if the Band/ community has their own form of dispute resolution services. With this information, CAS will discuss different methods, including First Nations approaches of ADR with the family. It is then the family's choice as to the form of ADR in which they would like to participate. There are also circumstances when approaches will be blended to better fit the needs of the individual family.

Section 17(3) states:

If a society or a person, including a child, who is receiving child welfare services proposes that an alternative dispute resolution method or process referred to in subsection (1) or (2) be undertaken to assist in resolving an issue relating to a child or a plan for the child's care, the Children's Lawyer may provide legal representation to the child if, in the opinion of the Children's Lawyer, such legal representation is appropriate.

When a referral is made for ADR, a referral must also be sent to the Office of the Children's Lawyer (OCL) in Toronto, Ontario. A representative from the OCL will then determine if it is beneficial to appoint a lawyer to represent the child in the ADR process. This will be discussed in more detail in "The Process" section.

Section 17(4) states:

If a society makes or receives a proposal that an alternative dispute resolution method or process referred to in subsection (1) or (2) be undertaken under subsection (3) in a matter involving a First Nations, Inuk or Métis child, the society shall give notice of the proposal to a representative chosen by each of the child's Bands and First Nations, Inuit or Métis communities.

If the ADR process has begun for a child who identifies as First Nations, Inuit or Métis, the Society must notify the child's Band or First Nations community. The Band may then reach out to the family to provide additional support to the family if the family consents.

ONTARIO RISK ASSESSMENT MODEL

In 1997, a decision was made to implement a common risk assessment tool across Ontario. The Ontario Risk Assessment Model (ORAM) was designed as a standardized, comprehensive approach to the assessment of risk across all CAS agencies. ORAM's primary goal was to promote and support a structured and rational decision-making approach to case practice, without replacing professional judgement. The specific tools included in

ORAM were intended to help workers design strategies to reduce risk, and build on family strengths.

ORAM had seven key components:

1. Eleven Risk Decision Points
- i. Does the case meet eligibility requirements for child welfare services?
- ii. What is the response time?
- iii. Is the child safe now?
- iv. Are the child protection concerns verified?
- v. Is the child in need of protection?
- vi. Is the child at risk of future abuse or neglect?
- vii. What other assessment issues must be considered to inform the plan of service?
- viii. What is the plan of service for the child and family?
- ix. Does the case continue to meet eligibility requirements for child protection service?
- x. Have assessments changed?
- xi. Should the plan of service be modified?

2. Standards to Guide Each Decision Point

These were new standards for each risk decision, and were designed to provide support and consistency for decisions made for each child protection case.

3. Eligibility Assessment

Child protection staff use the *Eligibility Spectrum* at the time of the referral to make decisions about the eligibility for service. The *Eligibility Spectrum* helps CAS staff to consistently interpret the need for child protection intervention.

4. Safety Assessment and Immediate Planning

The child protection worker completes the *Safety Assessment* at the first face-to-face contact with a child following a new or subsequent referral that requires investigation. When immediate safety interventions are required to ensure the child's safety while the investigation continues, an *Immediate Safety Intervention Plan* is completed.

5. Risk Assessment

The child protection worker uses their knowledge of Risk Assessment during the investigation phase and on an ongoing basis to assess the likelihood of future harm to the child. The child protection worker completes the *Risk Assessment Tool* when the assessment determines that a child is in need of protection and for subsequent case reviews.

6. Assessment of Other Child Protection Issues

The child protection worker completes an assessment of child protection issues to ensure that all issues related to the child's best interests, protection and well-being are addressed. It includes such subject areas as child development, and long-term parenting capacity.

7. Plan of Service Connected to the Risk Assessment of Other Child Protection Issues

The child protection worker, while completing the Risk Assessment and the assessment of other child protection issues, and involving relevant parties, identifies issues to be addressed in the

43

Plan of Service. The child protection worker determines outcomes required to reduce harm and risk of harm, and establishes strategies for achieving those outcomes. In this way, the information from the investigation and assessment process is linked directly to the planned interventions contained in the Plan of Service.

Although ORAM is no longer practiced, there are elements of the model that remain in use today including but not limited to:

- Eligibility Spectrum (updated)
- Safety Assessment (updated/ redesigned)
- Risk Assessment (updated/ redesigned)

BILL 210 (Differential Response)

On November 30, 2006, Bill 210 became part of the legislation in Ontario, and included several significant amendments to the CFSA. Other names used to reference the Bill were *Transformation Agenda*, and *Differential Response* (DR). Bill 210 aimed to achieve better outcomes for children and youth while promoting their safety, well-being, and permanency. The changes in CAS service delivery were designed to create:

- A more flexible and responsive intake and assessment model.
- A court process strategy to help reduce delays for children and youth and to promote alternatives to court through alternate dispute resolution methods
- A broader range of placement and intervention options to support early and effective permanency planning.

DR is a way of delivering child welfare services that allows greater flexibility than ORAM in the approach to child safety. DR is meant to be adaptable based on the presenting issues and needs, while still keeping the safety of the child at the forefront.

One of the big changes associated with DR was involving families more in the decision-making process, and encouraging a strengths-based approach to working with them. To be clear, DR was not implemented to forget about risk. It was introduced as a means to empower families and reduce risk. Part of the empowerment came from introducing ADR into the legislation.

ONTARIO REGULATION 496/ 06

This Regulation outlines criteria of the ADR process, but does not specifically list the prescribed processes. It indicates that the prescribed method of ADR must meet the following criteria:
- entered into with consent of all participants
- the process can be terminated at any time by any of the participants
- conducted by an impartial facilitator with no decision-making authority
- must satisfy the Regulation's confidentiality requirements
- must not be an arbitration.

The confidentiality provisions of this Regulation are:
- nobody involved in the ADR process, including the facilitator can be asked to give evidence or produce documents in a civil proceeding about anything to do with the ADR process.

Note: Family court and court involving CAS are both considered civil court.

- none of the content of the ADR meetings is admissible in civil court:
    - → unless there are reasonable grounds to believe that someone may be at risk of harm (including Duty to Report if a child may be in need of protection).
    - → unless an individual consents to the disclosure of their own personal information
    - → the terms of an agreement, memorandum of understanding or plan arising out of the ADR may be shared with the court, and all lawyers for the participants
- the ADR facilitator may disclose non-identifying information for research or educational purposes, but the facilitator must inform the parties of this possibility prior to the ADR process beginning.
- the participants may discuss the content of ADR with their lawyer.

Many of the Agreements to Mediate in circulation today have these confidentiality provisions built in to ensure that the participants are made aware in advance of the joint mediation session.

POLICY DIRECTIVE: CW 005-06

The MCYS issued this Policy Directive effective November 30, 2006; the same day that Bill 210 came into law. There is currently a group working with MCYS to discuss changes to this directive. However, no formal changes have been implemented as of yet.

There is considerable overlap among contents of this Directive, Ontario Regulation 496/ 06, and the CYFSA. In this Directive however, there are key points not made elsewhere. This Directive specifically mentions the three prescribed forms of ADR to be used under the CYFSA, facilitator qualification criteria and impartiality, CAS record keeping with respect to ADR, and more.

CAS Record Keeping

CP Med is a closed process. That is to say that aside from the mediated agreement, none of the information from the process is made available outside of the meeting(s). CAS does however have specific obligations with respect to their reporting of CP Med. CAS is required to consider ADR in every case and once considered, they must keep a record of that consideration. They must also record the reasons they decided to move forward with ADR or not move forward with ADR. CAS must also track outcomes of the ADR process, and report back to MCYS on a quarterly basis.

Facilitator Impartiality

Ontario Regulation 496/ 06 requires ADR facilitators to be impartial, and have no decision-making authority. This policy further defines impartiality. There is also clarification as to when facilitators are also employed by a CAS.

When possible, the facilitator should be employed outside of a CAS; whether it be self-employment or through a different agency. When employed by a CAS, facilitators SHOULD have their own office, and when possible, have their ADR meetings at a location outside of CAS. If employed by a CAS, facilitators MUST:
- have a distinct role separate from the child protection role and the child welfare team

- not have access to client files or CAS database
- not have access to casenotes or court information
- not report to a child protection supervisor, and must report to senior management

ELIGIBILITY SPECTRUM

The *Eligibility Spectrum* is a tool designed to assist CAS staff in making consistent and accurate decisions about a family's eligibility for service at the time of referral. When CAS receives information about a child, the Eligibility Spectrum is used to code the referral based on the reason for service/ allegations, the level of severity, and response time. The referral coding can be deviated provided there is a reasonable explanation documented in the CAS file.

Referrals to the CAS are coded according to the following sections:

1. Physical/Sexual Harm by Commission
2. Harm By Omission
3. Emotional Harm
4. Abandonment/Separation
5. Caregiver Capacity
6. Request for Counselling
7. Request for Adoption Services
8. Family Based Care
9. Volunteer Services
10. Request for Assistance
11. Request for Youth Services

If the referral codes in Section One to Eight, it is then further scaled numerically. The second number is a more specific sub-category of the type of alleged maltreatment. Referrals are then given a letter designation to indicate the level of severity. The level of severity is what determines the response time. Referrals are coded as either a twelve hour response, a seven day response, or no response at all.

THE PROCESS

CONSENT & CONFIDENTIALITY

Prior to initiating the ADR referral, the worker must have consent of the parties. This is not a mandatory requirement of the mediation process per se, but it is a requirement of the Freedom of Information and Protection of Privacy Act (FIPPA). There are also provisions in the CYFSA that relate to confidentiality. It is critical that anyone facilitating CP Med be aware of the legislations that relate to confidentiality in their jurisdiction.

The section of FIPPA that most applies to CP Med and mediation in general is Section 21.1(a), and it states:

> A head shall refuse to disclose personal information to any person other than the individual to whom the information relates except,
> a) upon the prior written request or consent of the individual, if the record is one to which the individual is entitled to have access;

In the CYFSA, valid consent is covered in Section 21(2), and it states:

> A person's consent or revocation of a consent or participation in or termination of an agreement under this Act is valid if, at the time the consent is given or revoked or the agreement is made or terminated, the person,
>
> a) has capacity;
> b) is reasonably informed as to the nature and consequences of the consent or agreement, and of alternatives to it;

c) gives or withdraws the consent or executes the agreement or notice of termination voluntarily, without coercion or undue influence; and
d) has had a reasonable opportunity to obtain independent advice.

As a result of these sections of the FIPPA and the CYFSA, CAS cannot give the mediator ANY information about a client without consent of the client. It is very frustrating to call a client to initiate an intake appointment, only to find out they have no idea that a mediation referral has been made. In the event that CAS does release the client's information without consent, the FIPPA views this as an "invasion of privacy."

As a result, the mediator should ensure that at the very least, the CAS has received verbal consent from the clients for CAS to share their information with the mediator. Information to be shared includes but is not limited to:
- name(s)
- contact information
- file history

In the event that the mediator receives confidential client information and consent has not been provided, the information should be destroyed prior to review by the mediator.

One way to avoid delays in service and confusion is to provide the local CAS with copies of a Consent to ADR template. On the consent form, the following should be included:
- space for the client's name and contact information
- an effective date and an expiration date
- that the client is consenting to their information being disclosed to the mediator, the local TPA, and the OCL
- a revocability clause

Reasons for these items include:

Space for the client's name and contact information → to help ensure information provided is for the correct client

Effective Date and Expiration Date → an expiration date is helpful so the client understands that information is not available indefinitely. It also provides an opportunity to inform the client that families often return to ADR for assistance. If this occurs within the suggested timelines, the process can proceed more quickly as updated consents are not required.

Consent for information to be shared with the mediator, the local TPA, and OCL → The mediator's information only applies in jurisdictions where CAS contacts the mediator directly. In jurisdictions where the TPA assigns the cases, the mediator is covered under that organization's umbrella.

OCL should be included as well. OCL needs to be notified when an ADR referral is made. Clients need to know with whom their information is being shared. It also creates an opportunity for CAS to explain that OCL may appoint a lawyer to represent the child, thus preventing the possibility of future anxiety when the client receives a phone call from a lawyer.

Revocability Clause → This reminds clients that the process is voluntary, and they have the ability to withdraw at anytime.

Ideally, CAS should ask the family member to sign a consent form like the example in *Appendix A*. Although verbal consent is sufficient, best practice is to have a signed consent form. The form can then be uploaded to the file, to confirm that the participant consented. This is important for the worker if the file is ever audited. It is also a clear indication that ADR was considered on the file. Depending on the TPA and/ or the mediator, sometimes the signed consent form will be included with the CP Med referral.

When clients consent to ADR, the consent should be one-directional. They are consenting to their information being disclosed to the mediator by CAS. The mediator should not be disclosing information to CAS about the client (outside of Duty To Report) and as a result, the consent to ADR should not include a provision for the mediator to share information with CAS. In order for the mediator to disclose any personal information about the clients to anyone (including CAS), the clients must consent ahead of time. If this is necessary, the mediator should have a conversation with the client ahead of time to explain why the information sharing is necessary. If the mediator discloses personal information without consent, this is again viewed as breach of confidentiality.

CHILDREN 12 AND OLDER

When making a referral for ADR, many CAS' require the child to sign a consent if the child is twelve years of age or older. This is specific to each agency and TPA. It is not mandatory according to the CYFSA, Policy Directive CW 005-06, or Ontario Regulation 496/ 06. Of note however, Section 23(1) of the CYFSA states:

A service provider may provide a counselling service to a child who is 12 or older with the child's consent, and no other person's consent is required, but if the child is younger than 16, the service provider shall discuss with the child at the earliest appropriate opportunity the desirability of involving the child's parent.

Although ADR is not counselling, it can be seen as a therapeutic process for children and families. As a result, best practice is to have any person twelve years of age or older sign a consent to release their information for the purposes of ADR.

It is however necessary to get consent from the child if they are sixteen (16) years old or older. This is covered in Section 22(1) of the CYFSA. Further, a child who is sixteen (16) or older may enter into the CP Med process without parental consent if CAS believes they are a child in need of protection. Reminder, CAS would likely not have an active file if they did not believe the child was in need of protection. Section 22(1) of the CYFSA states:

a service provider may provide a service to a person who is 16 or older only with the person's consent, except where the court orders under this Act that the service be provided to the person.

REFERRAL

Anyone may suggest ADR on an open CAS file. That includes workers, family members, and lawyers. Currently, there is not a mechanism in place for families to make a CP Med referral, nor is there one for lawyers. The responsibility of making the referral is typically tasked to the assigned workers on the consent of the parties.

It is the local TPA that sets the referral process, and the referral is filtered through them in some way. The referral process varies from location to location. For example, the referral process in Toronto is very different than the referral process in Peterborough which is also different than the referral process in Belleville.

Some CAS agencies send the referral to the local TPA who then assigns the case to a mediator. That mediator may be selected as they are next on the roster to receive a case, or they may have been requested to be the mediator. Other CAS agencies send the referral directly to the mediator. In some instances, the worker must get approval from the local TPA prior to proceeding with the mediation referral. They are then required to find their own CP mediator.

There is also variation in the referral form. Some TPA's ask the worker to fill out a referral form specific to that TPA. Others use the "Office of the Children's Lawyer Notice of ADR" referral form. In some areas, the worker only needs to phone the mediator to initiate the process. If you are considering CP Med as a practice, be sure to check with the local TPA for their policies and processes, and make sure you are able to practice on their roster before accepting a CP Med file. Some rosters in the province are closed, and are not accepting additional mediators.

OFFICE OF THE CHILDREN'S LAWYER

The Office of the Children's Lawyer (OCL) is a division of the Ministry of the Attorney General (MAG). The OCL represents children under the age of eighteen (18) in court cases involving custody and access and child protection. They will also represent children in civil, estates, and trusts cases. The OCL employs both lawyers and clinicians (typically social workers), who work on a fee-for-service basis across the province.

As per Policy Directive CW 005-06, CAS <u>must</u> notify the OCL when they make a referral for ADR. If a lawyer is not currently involved to represent the child, CAS is required to use the prescribed referral form as shown in *Appendix B*. After reviewing the OCL Referral form, the OCL will then decide whether or not to appoint a lawyer for the child with respect to the ADR. It is not uncommon for a representative from the OCL to consult with the worker and/ or the mediator in making that determination. Once a determination is made, a representative from the OCL will notify the worker of the decision and oftentimes, the mediator as well.

There are also instances when a lawyer has already been appointed to represent the child. This typically occurs when a protection case is before the court, and a lawyer has been appointed to represent the child in that forum. If that is the case, the worker has an obligation to inform the assigned children's lawyer that the referral for mediation has been submitted. It is not necessary for the worker to send the prescribed Notice of ADR to the OCL in these instances.

Note: If a lawyer is representing a child in court, discussion needs to happen with the lawyer before the ADR referral is submitted to ensure that the lawyer (and their client) consent to the process being initiated; much like the adult parties.

When meeting with the family to discuss CP Med and ask for consent, the worker should inform the family that a referral will also be made to the OCL as part of the process.

There is some confusion as to which types of CP Med cases require OCL notification. At this time, all ADR referrals require OCL notification. It does not matter the child's age, type of case, or whether or not there is court involvement. If the mediator receives a CP Med referral in which an OCL referral has not been made, the mediator should direct the worker to notify the OCL as soon as possible; whether it be completing the prescribed form or contacting a lawyer already assigned to represent the child in another matter.

If the mediator believes it would be beneficial for the OCL to appoint a lawyer to represent the child in a CP Med, the mediator should contact the OCL directly, and inform them of their thoughts and reasons.

As noted earlier, there is currently a working group reviewing Policy Directive CW 005-06. As part of that process, the OCL notification requirements are being reviewed, and it is possible that some changes to the notification process will result.

SCREENING

Screening is an ongoing process in mediation and in CP Med, it begins as soon as the referral is received. At one time, mediators primarily screened for domestic violence only. Furthermore, if there was a history of physical violence in the relationship, mediation was automatically screened out. Victims of violence spoke out however, and they informed mediators that automatically screening them out was victimizing them again. An outside person was dictating whether or not they were allowed to advocate for themselves, and this was the same kind of oppression many of them experienced in their relationships. We've come a long way since then and thankfully, screening is now a much more in-depth process.

Nowadays, physical abuse is but one element that mediators are exploring in the screening process. Other areas being explored include, but are not limited to:
- verbal/ emotional abuse
- harassment
- sexual abuse/ assault
- financial abuse
- power and control
- coercion
- emotional readiness
- intellectual capacity

If CAS is aware of any of the aforementioned circumstances, the worker should include the information in the initial CP Med referral. That said, many clients are fearful that their children will be apprehended if they tell CAS and as a result, they may not disclose all of the relevant information to their worker. Therefore, screening must be done with everyone. The mediator should also be aware that new information can present itself at anytime in the process, and you need to be able to think quickly in order to deal with these dynamic situations.

There are many different family mediation screening tools in circulation, and different mediators have their preferences. When conducting a custody and access CP Med, it may be helpful to use a screening tool to further engage the client, and learn more about the family dynamics. This should be done however, in a strategic and meaningful way.

Simply sending clients the screening questionnaire ahead of time without any family information has the potential to backfire. In some instances, the parties still live in the same residence and the mediator may not know this. There is also the possibility that the parties still have contact at access exchanges or children's sporting events. As a result, there could be situations of fear and intimidation when a person completes the screening tool, and all of this has the potential to put clients at increased risk of harm if they disclose current of past abuse in the questionnaire.

To reduce this risk, some mediators ask the clients to complete a demographic questionnaire prior to booking their intake appointment. Contained in the demographic questionnaire may be the client's name, address, children's information, a brief history of the relationship, and more. With this information, the mediator can then get a sense of some of the relationship dynamics. If they choose, the mediator can then be strategic with the order in which they meet with clients.

Generally speaking, these mediators will first meet with the alleged victim of abuse or the person with less negotiating power. This is so the mediator can do pre-emptive safety planning with that person before meeting with the other party. That pre-emptive safety planning may relate to the design of a safe joint mediation session or a safe termination process. Ultimately, if the mediation does not move forward, termination needs to occur in a way that there is no perceived blame. This will be covered in more detail in the "Safe Termination" section, but it is also part of the screening process.

Some safety steps in the intake process include, but are not limited to:
- do not disclose to dates/ times of intake appointments to others
- do not inform parties if they are the first/ last intake completed
- do not inform parties in the intake session that you feel mediation will move forward (this is especially important if there are more intakes to complete)

A significant limitation to using a screening tool in CP Med is that a large percentage of the child welfare population has literacy challenges. It would often serve no purpose to send clients a screening tool ahead of time, because they may not be able to read it. Also, many of our clients do not have access to computers or printers. For all of these reasons, if you are planning to use a screening tool, it may make more sense to complete it with the client during their intake appointment.

The screening process is further complicated by the fact that CAS is one of the clients in the CP Med process. As a result of their authority, there is often an inherent power imbalance between CAS and family members. Given the various dynamics, traditional Family Mediation screening tools would not be effective with respect to CAS. Also, it is highly unlikely that mediation would be suggested if there was an incident of abuse involving a worker. In those cases, the matter would most likely be in criminal court.

Screening is multi-layered. Although part of the process is to learn if there have been any incidents of abuse or significant power imbalances, the mediator is also screening for emotional readiness and intellectual capacity. Ultimately, the goal of the screening process is to determine if there are any challenges and if so, to ensure that all of the parties are able to actively participate in the process without any fear or risk of harm. It should be clarified that harm can also include financial and emotional ramifications of a bad deal.

Nowadays, mediators are trained in creative ways to develop a process in which the parties can feel safe, and actively participate. If the mediator has concerns about any of the items revealed during the screening process, they should explore ways to modify the process. This may include, but is not limited to:

- shuttle mediation
- support people (eg friend, service provider, lawyer, interpreter etc)
- delaying the joint mediation session to allow time for clients to move, get counselling etc
- shorter joint mediation sessions

To date, there are no screening tools specific to CP Med. Perhaps that is a direct result of the plethora of subject matter discussed in CP Med. Although we can use existing screening tools for custody and access cases, there remains a need for screening tools for other types of CP Meds. Given the volume of CP Med cases that are custody and access however, I highly recommend mediators take a screening-specific refresher course every few years.

NARRATIVE:

The parties included CAS, Dad, Granddad, and OCL. Dad had gone three years without contact with his children or Granddad. This was a direct result of charges of uttering threats towards all of them. He spent a brief period of time in jail, and was then on probation. Much of this information was included in the initial CP Med referral.

Mum had not been involved with the children for approximately ten years. The children had been apprehended from her care, and placed with Dad provided he lived with Granddad. Mum eventually stopped attending court, and Dad and Granddad were awarded joint custody. They lived together for many years, and then the aforementioned incident occurred.

Dad happened to be the last intake I completed. Even from my first phone call with him, I could tell he would be challenging. Almost immediately, he became emotional, and described himself as a "Learning Disabled Adult." He had recently broken up with a girlfriend, and was now living in a rooming house. Before that, this man in his 40's had never lived alone.

Dad was very challenging to keep on track during his intake. He was very melancholy, and when he did emote, it was extreme sadness. He reported being incredibly overwhelmed by the simplest of tasks, and described days of sitting in a chair looking out the window wondering why he was put on this earth. In his words, "I feel like I've been put here to suffer." During his intake, it was also abundantly clear that Dad loved his children and his father.

I was not in court, and do not have all of the facts, so I cannot say whether or not our justice system failed Dad with his conviction. I can safely say however, that our community support system failed him after his release from jail. He was in jail in a small town and upon release, he remained in that small town. He had no friends, no family close by, and perhaps most important, he had absolutely no supports.

Although the case appeared suitable for mediation, it was clear to me that Dad was not a good candidate on his own for mediation.

When I asked if he felt he was able to participate in the process, he said "No." To me, it would only be possible for him to participate (and to have a relationship with his children) with some kind of support system. To conduct a mediation with him having no supports felt underhanded, and it would be a disservice to him, Granddad, and the children.

After meeting with Dad, I took it upon myself to seek out supports in his community. I mentioned this to him during his appointment, and he was very appreciative. I first contacted John Howard Society, and gave them a synopsis of his situation without giving any identifying information. They agreed to work with me to find some supports for Dad, connected him with new-to-him clothing, and also looked into an Adult Protection Worker for him. In time, this Dad may be able to participate in mediation but at the time of referral, my role was to put him in touch with someone who could help him with daily living.

As of the release date of this book, this mediation file remains open.

Shuttle Mediation

As part of the intake process, the mediator should always explore whether or not the parties will be able to manage in the same room. It is very common for parties to say "I don't want to sit in the same room with them." The mediator has a responsibility to explore this further. Not wanting to be in the same room as a preference is not the same as needing to be in a different room out of fear or safety. Once you dig deeper, a decision can be made as to whether or not a shuttle mediation is more fitting.

UNCOMFORTABLE IS THE NOT THE SAME AS UNSAFE

In custody and access mediations in particular, it is sometimes our job to break down barriers so that parties can work together as parents. I'm amazed at how many people come to my office that haven't been in the same room together for years simply out of hurt feelings. In my opinion, hurt feelings are not reason enough to do a shuttle mediation.

In a compassionate way, our clients occasionally need to be encouraged to sit in the same room and talk. One way to break down these barriers is to remind clients that they will not be left alone in a room, and they can take breaks at anytime. They also have the ability to meet privately with the mediator at anytime. Part of our job is to remind them that they are parents first, and former partners second. Of course, safety is paramount and if there is any risk to safety, including intimidation, a shuttle mediation is suggested.

CONTACT RESTRICTIONS

Restrictions refer to Restraining Orders, Peace Bonds, Bail Conditions, Probation Orders, etc. It is incredibly important to know if there are any legal restrictions in place preventing any of the parties from having contact with one another. One reason is that legal restrictions may be related to a incident of violence between the parties. The contact restrictions provides the mediator with an opportunity to ask questions about the incident, thus learning more about how to keep people safe in the mediation process.

The conversation about contact restrictions should be had with each family member, and CAS during their respective intake appointments. In the event that there are contact restrictions in place, workers often have a copy of the conditions in their file. If possible, review the conditions and discuss whether or not a variance is required. If so, ask the worker to assist the family with the process of getting a variance. It is also helpful if the worker writes a letter to the necessary person (e.g. Probation Officer, Crown Attorney, etc), supporting a variance for the purposes of CP Med.

If there are legal conditions that the parties not communicate, there is a possibility that one or both of the parties may be charged if they continue in mediation. It is the responsibility of the parties to have the conditions varied by whomever imposed the conditions. Keep in mind that shuttle mediation still counts as "indirect contact," and could result in charges if certain restrictions are not in place.

The parties cannot simply inform the mediator that they consent to varying the conditions. Without legal documentation confirming that the conditions have been varied, the mediator must operate as if the conditions remain in place and are enforceable. Best practice is to request a copy of the conditions and any variance for the file.

NARRATIVE:

A well-respected mediator ran into a predicament with respect to no-contact conditions during a mediation. During the intake phase, the mediator learned of current no-contact conditions between the parties. The mediator informed the clients that prior to moving forward with the mediation, the conditions needed to be varied to allow for mediation. Both parties indicated that they were comfortable moving ahead with the mediation without varying the conditions. In spite of this, the mediator insisted.

The parties consulted with their lawyers, and the lawyers subsequently contacted the mediator. Both lawyers agreed that it was ok to proceed with the mediation and in fact, both lawyers attended the mediation.

As with most mediations, there was a moment of heightened emotionality. At that time, one of the parties left the office, and subsequently called police. As a result, the other person was arrested for breaching their conditions.

The lesson here is that regardless of whether or not the clients and their lawyers agree to work cooperatively, their word does not trump a court condition. If there are any legal conditions in place, they should be varied prior to the joint mediation session to avoid the possibility of further court or police involvement.

NARRATIVE:

As part of my usual intake process, I enquired as to whether or not there were any legal contact restrictions. All of the parties (CAS, and each parent) informed me that there was a restraining order in the past, but nothing current. They all informed me that once there was a court order, there was no longer a restraining order.

All of the parties also indicated that the parents only communicated by email. This did not raise any alarm bells, because it is very common for family engaged in high conflict to communicate via email. It wasn't until my last intake that I saw the existing court order. One of the paragraphs read:

The parties shall not communicate with one another directly or indirectly except for the purpose of arranging access or relating to an issue relating to the child. Any communication between the parties with respect to the child shall be in writing through e-mail.

Unfortunately, there was no other wording in their court order with respect to a Future Dispute Resolution process, communication through a third party, or mediation. As a result, legally, these parents could only communicate via email. Although I could have technically run the mediation with them in separate rooms and emailing me their information, I thought it safest to request a variance to their court order to allow for mediation. I suggested wording such as:

- ...through email except for the purposes of mediation
- ...through email, or through a mutually agreed upon third (3rd) party
- ... through email, or through the Children's Aid Society

Once their court order was amended, we moved forward with the joint mediation session. Although it created significant time delays, there was no risk that someone would end up in jail as a result of participating in mediation.

Note: The wording "or through the Children's Aid Society" is allowable as the ADR process is referred by the CAS, and overseen by MCYS.

LOCATION! LOCATION! LOCATION!

The concept of safety is defined by everyone involved. That includes the clients, and the mediator. When designing the mediation sessions, you are not creating an environment free of conflict. Rather, you are responsible for creating an environment where people can express their feelings, wants and needs and not feel attacked in the process. This begins by choosing a location in which all of the participants will feel safe.

When ADR first rolled out in 2006, the expectation was that none of the mediation appointments were to be held at the CAS office. The worry about having appointments at the CAS office was the perception that the mediator may have been aligned with the CAS and not impartial. There was also a worry of clients feeling intimidated by having meetings at the CAS office. Over time however, the thinking around this issue has evolved.

Some clients reported that meeting at a different location actually created increased stress for them. They already knew where the CAS office was located, and had experience with finding transportation to that location. This is especially important when working with clients who struggle to process new information. So, in some instances, meeting at the CAS office can actually reduce potential stress for families. As mediators, our role is to help families; not create added stress.

Ideally, mediation sessions are scheduled at a neutral location, and away from the courthouse, CAS offices, or offices of the parties' lawyers. As noted, exceptions to this can be made on consent of the parties, but the mediator must take special care to ensure the parties are agreeing of their own will, and not due to pressure from others. That includes pressure from the mediator to hold the joint mediation session at their location of preference.

Currently, many mediators facilitate CP Med at the CAS office. This is often a result of mediators servicing multiple communities. In those situations, renting offices in several communities is simply not financially feasible. It is also worth considering rural Ontario where population density is lower. As a result, there may not be enough demand to justify renting a fixed office location in those communities.

If mediators are holding meetings with family members at CAS offices, mediators need to inform participants that CAS is only being used as a result of space availability and not because of any alliance with CAS. Further, if a participant is not comfortable meeting at the CAS office, the mediator needs to make arrangements to meet the participants elsewhere. Other possible meeting locations include but are not limited to:

- churches
- libraries
- lawyers offices
- other professional office spaces

Occasionally, participants will ask to meet at a local restaurant. A public location like a restaurant is not ideal due to the confidential and emotional nature of the conversation. If the clients insists however, an intake appointment could be held in a public setting. There are even instances when intake appointments could be facilitated outside. Ultimately, the goal is to make the participant feel comfortable with the process, gain their trust, and gather the necessary information required to determine if the mediation will proceed.

Upon occasion, participants will ask to meet in their home. In Family Group Conferencing/ Decision-Making, the expectation is that the facilitator meet with the family members in their home or a location of their choosing. Prior to client contact however, the facilitator has met with the CAS, and has an understanding of the family dynamics and who the participants are. From that information, they are able to make important decisions about where to meet participants, and ensure facilitator safety. If the client is the first person with whom you are meeting, meeting in their home is strongly discouraged. There is insufficient information to ensure your safety.

*YOUR OWN SAFETY
IS YOUR FIRST PRIORITY!*

INTAKE

SCHEDULING

It is important to maintain neutrality throughout the entire mediation process. Because the referral comes from the worker, they are usually the first point of contact. As a result, their intake appointment is often scheduled first. To be clear, this does not always mean that the worker is the first person seen. It simply means they are *often* the first person contacted. As a general rule, I contact the participants in the order in which their contact information is listed on the referral. All appointments are based strictly on calendar availability; not their identified title or role. The order in which intakes are completed should not matter.

There are some mediators who believe that they should meet with the worker first. I disagree! If the default is to meet with the worker first, the perception to clients may be that the CAS information is the most important information for the mediator to receive. Some mediators believe they should meet with the worker first so the mediator may share why CAS is involved or why CAS believes mediation would be helpful. Again, I disagree with this. It is neither the mediator's role nor their responsibility to share that information. It is the worker's responsibility. All intake appointments must be treated as confidential. It is the same concept as a Family Mediation. A mediator should not disclose any content from the other client's intake appointment. In CP Med, a worker is a client, just as a family member is a client.

The Ontario CP Med Manual (2006) states that family members should be met before CAS workers. Again, I disagree. The reason it is recommended to meet with family members first is because of the inherent power imbalance that exists between CAS and family members. Although there may be a perceived power differential between CAS and a family, there are many dynamics to consider when assessing power. This may include experience of the worker, strength of individual personalities, or merits of the child protection case. Another point to consider is which of the family members are met first, because there are often several family members involved.

It is important that all parties, including CAS, see the mediator as neutral and impartial. Strategically meeting with a certain identified group (ie worker, mother, father, parent, client, etc) first has the potential to create a perceived bias. Actual bias is not as important as perceived bias. How clients perceive the mediator and the process will dictate how they interact with the mediator and the process.

YOUR PERCEPTION IS EQUAL TO YOUR REALITY
- Raymond Hayes -

TECHNOLOGY

Technology dominates our world! There are smart phones, tablets, computers, internet TV's, countless apps, and more. Many professionals use technology in their everyday practice, and this is also true in child welfare. It has also worked its way into CP Med. That said, there is some debate about the use of technology during CP Med appointments.

There are some who believe technology is a more efficient, environmentally-friendly method of note-taking. Others however, believe that the use of technology further marginalizes clients as the families may not be able to afford the same luxuries. This may create further obstacles for the mediator in designing a safe, power-neutral mediation environment. If your preference is to hand-write your notes on paper, you may find it helpful to scan your notes for digital filing. By doing so and shredding the originals, you're able to save a lot of storage space.

Some mediators use writing applications on tablets to take notes during intake appointments. The information is then automatically backed up. At the end of the year, files can be saved to an external storage device, and locked in a safe place. If you chose to use such a practice, ensure that files are backed up in more than one location (ie "the cloud," external storage, separate computer, etc). Just as paper can get lost, so too can digital files.

Although technology can be intimidating to some, there are other who will find it intriguing when they meet with the mediator. It is important for the mediator to be attentive to this and if necessary, open to the idea of making adjustments on a case-by-case basis.

It is not recommended that the mediator use a computer to type out their notes during an intake appointment with a family member, unless the mediator is very skilled at maintaining a personal connection while doing so. Most people are familiar with various clinicians writing during appointments, and are used to it. Whether on a tablet or paper, the clinician is still writing. Typing on a computer however, may be seen as impersonal.

An exception to this may be when meeting with other service providers such as CAS. Like mediators, they are in an environment where there is lots of note-taking. As a result, they often understand that sometimes, efficiency is necessary. Regardless, be attentive to the reactions of your note-taking methods and adjust accordingly.

If technology is used to review certain documentation, ensure that a paper copy is available to clients as well. This is especially important if it is a document that the party will sign. If you do not have a paper copy present, offer to send a copy to the party after the appointment, if the client wishes.

Communication is another area which has been greatly impacted by technology. For decades, email has become a norm for communication. In the last ten years, text messaging has increased dramatically. More and more, people are disconnecting their home phones as they rely on cell phones. Also increasing is the number of people with cell phones with limited talk-time, or only a text messaging plan.

As a result, there are some clients that are only able to schedule appointments via text message. If this is the case, the mediator should set clear boundaries about how and when text messaging will be used. It is also beneficial to have a cell phone dedicated strictly to work. Clients are inclined to text at anytime of the day or night and if the mediator is using their personal cell phone, they may be inclined to engage in client-contact outside of their business hours. This may then have a negative impact on both self-care, and family. It is the mediator's responsibility to set boundaries on their practice.

CONFIDENTIALITY AGREEMENT

As discussed, CP Med is covered by the regulations, policy directives, and legislation associated with the CYFSA. Many of our clients however, are not aware of this information. As a means of sharing this necessary information, I ask clients to sign a confidentiality agreement at the beginning of their intake appointment. I use this document as a tool for explaining the process. It helps set the tone for the meetings, and lets people know that their information is safe with the mediator.

Appendix C shows a standard Confidentiality Agreement. Below is a breakdown of the document, and an explanation of what is included:

1. *Mediation is a voluntary process, and any participant has the right to withdraw from the process at any time.*

Clients need to know that the process is voluntary. Many clients attend mediation thinking it is a mandatory process in which they must engage. When asked what they would like to get out of mediation, it is not uncommon to hear "CAS told me I have to come." Even though the worker may have only suggested ADR, because the suggestion came from CAS, clients often feel it is mandatory. The same can be said about judges making the "suggestion."

2. *The mediator was an employee of the Hastings Children's Aid Society until July 4, 2011. The mediator is no longer an employee of the Hastings Children's Aid Society and as such, does not have access to the family's child welfare history beyond what is disclosed in the mediation process.*

As someone who once worked as a Child Protection Worker, I am very aware that not all clients like CAS. There are also those who believe that the system is stacked against them. To me, it is very important that I inform clients of any potential conflicts of interests right away. I also use this as an opportunity to inform them that I know the child welfare system, and may be able to take time to explain why certain events happen when working with CAS. Clients appreciate the honesty. I have conducted hundreds of child welfare mediations, and have not had a client refuse service yet as a result of my CAS background.

3. *The mediator will not voluntarily disclose any verbal and/ or written communication that takes place during this meeting. The following exceptions apply:*
- *Disclosure for my lawyer or third party advisors;*

- *Where information suggests an actual or perceived threat to human life and/ or safety (notify CAS for a child, notify Police for an adult);*
- *Where ordered to do so by law;*
- *Research and/ or educational purposes (non-identifying information);*
- *On written consent*

These are standard confidentiality clauses, but clients need to know where their information will and will not go. Further, these are items included in Section 2 of Ontario Regulation 496/ 06.

4. *I consent to the presence of language interpreters, mediation interns and/ or assistants for the purposes of professional training. All such observers and/ or participants are also bound by the same rules of confidentiality as the mediator as outlined in Paragraph 3.*

When working in larger, more culturally diverse communities, it is not uncommon for interpreters to be present for meetings. Also, many mediators have observers and interns connected with their practice. Clients need to understand that other individuals in the meeting must also keep the information confidential.

Some clients are not be comfortable with the idea of an intern or observer being present for their appointments. If an intern or observer is going to be present, ensure the clients are aware ahead of time. Also, give clients the opportunity to decline the presence of an intern or observer if that is the client's preference.

5. *I shall not record the content of any mediation appointments through any means such as audio, video etc.*

In my years as a protection worker, I had several clients record conversations. As a result, there remains worry that conversations may be recorded in the child welfare mediation process. If I become aware that a client is recording our conversations and/ or meetings, I will terminate the meeting. There is only one reason a client would record a conversation, and that is to use it as evidence in the future. Child Protection Mediation is a closed process and as such, none of the information, aside from the Memorandum of Understanding, is to be used in any future civil proceeding.

I also use this as an opportunity to inform workers and clients that only the mediator may take notes during the joint mediation session(s). This will be covered in further detail in the Joint Mediation Session section.

6. *I shall not summons nor otherwise require the mediator to testify and/or produce records and/ or notes in any current or future civil proceedings.*

This informs people that information shared with the mediator is not going to make its way into any court documents.

I acknowledge that I have read the Confidentiality Agreement or had it read to me, and understand this agreement.

Many of the clients I work with have literacy challenges. This may be a result of education, trauma, or developmental challenges. Regardless of the reason, it exists. As a result, I read all documents to my clients, and explain each paragraph in everyday language. This way, I believe the information is understood, and the client does not feel marginalized due to possible literacy challenges. Policy Directive CW 005-06 indicates that:

"a written confidentiality agreement could act as a disincentive to certain persons to engaging in a prescribed method of ADR. In these cases, the minimum expectation is that children's aid societies only engage in a prescribed method of ADR where the elements of the confidentiality regulation are clearly communicated to participants by the ADR facilitator at the outset of the process."

By explaining the content of the agreement(s) with the clients, including the confidentiality clauses, the participants are still entering into an approved form of child welfare ADR.

FAMILY MEMBER

Everything we talk about today is completely confidential, and just between you and me. Exceptions to that would be if I think someone is at risk of harm. Then I have to report it. So, if I think you are going to hurt yourself or someone else, I need to make a phone call.

I also make sure that everyone I work with knows that I used to be a CAS Worker. I'm not anymore, and haven't been for about _____ years, but I like to make sure everyone knows where I came from. If it's an issue, we can talk about it. If not, we'll just keep going.

This is a pretty standard introduction that I use at the beginning of an intake appointment with family members. I immediately highlight confidentiality, Duty To Report, and potential conflict of interest. My hope is that by covering these details in the introduction, I avoid any surprises or misunderstandings of my role later in the meeting. Clients often want to start telling their story right away, but it is important to explain Duty To Report obligations before receiving any personal information.

After the mediator introduces themselves, explain the process to the participant. Clients need to be made aware that just because they want to do mediation, it does not mean it will automatically move forward. Part of the intake process is screening to ensure that the people and the case dynamics are appropriate for CP Med.

Clients often ask why mediation may not move forward. Do not tell them! If they are made aware of what the mediator is looking for, they may modify their answers based on their desire to participate in mediation or to not participate. A way around that is to tell clients that mediation will move forward if the mediator feels they can be of assistance to the family, and keep everyone safe physically and emotionally.

Although the decision to screen a case out of mediation may happen early in the process, it is important not to officially make the determination until all of the parties, including CAS, have been met. Waiting helps to avoid perceived blame. No reason given to the parties as to why mediation has not moved forward. Explain that if the group is given a reason, it lays blame, and that is not helpful. Also, all of the information gathered by the mediator up until that point is confidential, and cannot be shared. It saves a lot of stress for the mediator and confusion for the parties if this is clarified early in the intake process.

Appendix D shows a standard form that I use during an intake appointment with a family member. There are certain common questions that I ask, so I created a template to remind me to gather that information.

CULTURE

Understanding cultural differences is incredibly important for a multitude of reasons. It will help the mediator facilitate a more balanced process, and will also educate you as to the similarities and differences in your community. One specific question that should be asked is whether or not the child identifies as "First Nations, Inuit or Métis," as they are entitled to Indigenous Alternative Dispute Resolution (IADR) processes as discussed earlier. Although the worker should have provided this information earlier, it is not a question that is asked of all families.

This question also highlights cultural sensitivity. Terminology is always changing. In the past, the terms "Indian" & "Native" were common terms used when discussing individuals of First Nations descent. In fact, as of 2018, the Indian Act remains as the legislation to address concerns and rights of First Nations people. Although the legislative language of the Indian Act uses the terms Indian and Native, it is important to have conversations with people of different ethnic groups to ask what terminology they prefer. When meeting with someone of a different cultural group than yourself, ask them for their preferred terminology. For example, some people prefer the terms "Indigenous" or "First Nations." Also, give the participants permission to correct you with respect to terminology if it is something they find offensive. That demonstrates an openness to learn, and people generally respect that

INDEPENDENT LEGAL ADVICE

The mediator should know if the client has a lawyer, or has received Independent Legal Advice (ILA). If the client has not received ILA, the mediator has a responsibility to encourage the client to seek ILA. As a parent involved with CAS, they have certain rights and responsibilities. A lawyer is the best person to inform the clients of these items. If the client has retained a lawyer, there may be an expense for any conversation between the lawyer and the mediator. As a result, the mediator should ask the client if the mediator has permission to contact the lawyer. Although you may not always need to speak with the client's lawyer, it's better to have permission to call in the event that a conversation is necessary.

COURT:

Knowing whether or not the matter is before the court can provide helpful information as to potential timelines, and level of cooperation between the parties. It is also helpful to know if the matter is in Family Court or CAS Court. If the matter is in CAS Court, there may be a sense of greater conflict between the family and CAS, or CAS has potentially used a more intrusive intervention (i.e. apprehension).

This is also a good opportunity to explain to family members about the possibility of a lawyer being appointed for the child. There are times when workers may not have informed family members of this. In those cases, it can be quite stressful for a person to receive a call from a lawyer, and not know the context. By informing them ahead of time, it helps to reduce surprises and potential anxiety.

INTERVIEW CHILDREN:

In recent years, there has been a shift to include the child's voice in the mediation process. This will be covered later in the chapter "Voice of the Child." If the mediator is a proponent of a child-inclusive mediation process, it should be discussed with the parents/ caregivers of the child. Unless the child is in Extended Society Care, the mediator must have the permission of the parents/ caregivers to interview the child. If either parent does not consent, the mediator needs to have some discussion with the parents to understand their reasoning. This may have an impact as to whether or not the mediation moves forward.

Be sure to enquire about the ages of the children, and their overall well-being. The process is focussed on the best interests and safety of the children. The mediator should have some sense of how the children are doing, any behaviour or mental health challenges, and especially if the current situation is having an impact on them. Although the responses are often skewed to reflect the parent's position, the mediator will gain insight into the well-being of the children, and the relationship between the children and the parties.

HISTORY:

When meeting the family members, the mediator needs to understand the family's perspective as to why CAS is involved, and the dynamics between the different family members. You need to ensure each participant's intake appointment is treated as a blank canvas before starting. It is also critical that the mediator not share information from anyone else's intake appointment, including that of the CAS worker's intake appointment.

It is very common to have an image in your mind of the case dynamics based on one intake, only to have them completely changed by the end of the intake with another person. Leaving assumptions out of the meeting is critical to ensure that you understand the client's situation from the client's perspective. Perception is equal to reality, and how the client perceives the situation will have a tremendous impact on the mediation process.

STRENGTHS:

Many of the cases seen today in CP Med are custody and access cases. These files often have long-standing conflict, and the parties have become very entrenched in their opinions. If they are involved in litigation, there has also no doubt been documentation filed highlighting as many negative opinions as possible about each other. Asking about strengths of the other parties is a way to help parents shift their thinking. If the parent struggles to find a strength, ask them for a strength from the child's perspective.

MENTAL HEALTH:

As a result of TV and social media, the conversation of mental health is much more prevalent these days, but pop psychology is not new. Unfortunately, this also leads to a plethora of informal diagnoses. The most common ones I hear are Bi-Polar Disorder, Personality Disorder, and Post Traumatic Stress Disorder. Many people either diagnose themselves or the people around them without any real training or education on the matter.

That said, get a sense of everyone's mental health and any formal diagnoses. Be sure to ask the participants if there are any mental health concerns for themselves or the other party. If they offer a "diagnosis," follow up to discuss the symptomatology. It is not the mediator's role to diagnosis mental health, but having an understanding of client behaviours and attitudes will help the mediator to better manage the joint mediation session. The mediator also needs to enquire about any past or current treatment for the mental health concerns.

If an individual appears to be mentally and/ or emotionally unstable, mediation should not proceed at this time.

SUBSTANCE USE:

In our culture, substance use is becoming more common, and more acceptable. In the past, alcohol was the only acceptable substance to ingest, but with changing laws, marijuana use is also becoming more common. There is a growing opiate problem in different parts of the country. Regardless of the substance, the mediator should ask all of the participants if there are any concerns with respect to substance use for themselves or for the other party. If so, has there ever been or is there currently any treatment?

When dealing with substance use, the mediator should focus on the effect of the substance use on the child, and less on the actual substance itself. If the substance use is having a negative impact on the child, there is reason for concern. The mediator must be aware of the difference between recreational use and problem use, and hold their personal prejudices in check. They must also filter the information received to determine if the use is actually having a negative impact, or if the client is providing their own personal bias about substance use.

If either of the parties is actively using substances, and the substance is having a negative impact on the family dynamic, the mediator needs to have further discussions with the participants. Substance use can impact a person's ability to make good decisions, and affect them even when they are not under the influence. Under no circumstances should an intake or joint mediation session proceed if anyone appears to be impaired.

ADDICTION:

Although many people focus on substance use, there are many addictions from which a person can suffer. Addiction can be defined as a physiological and psychological dependence that is beyond voluntary control. It is an obsessive compulsion to which a person becomes powerless both physically and mentally. Even addictions that are not typically seen as physical (eg gambling, shopping etc), have a biological component as there is a neurochemical (dopamine) release in the brain during the activity. Dopamine is a neurotransmitter that helps control the brain's reward and pleasure centres.

Many addictions stem from a trauma background. Oftentimes, substance use is due to self-medicating traumatic symptoms. Pain may also be a factor in developing an addiction, as many opiate addictions begin from a doctor's prescription. The stigma and shame associated with addictions are a large reason why a person will try to hide their addiction.

Explore if there are any concerns with respect to addictions and if so, to what extent they impact the children and the parenting relationship. Examples of addiction include but are not limited to:

- drugs (prescription, non-prescription, inhalants)
- alcohol
- gambling (online, casino's, etc)
- sex or pornography
- food (emotional eating, binging and purging, etc)
- video games
- working
- exercise
- shopping

In the event that any of the parties discloses a past or present addiction, the mediator should explore if any treatment has been sought. If treatment occurred, there should be discussion about the type of treatment but more importantly, the effectiveness of the treatment.

Relapse is often considered a part of the recovery process, but attention should be placed on the long-term outcomes There are many types of substance abuse programs that offer medical treatments (eg methadone or suboxone for opiate addiction) but more often than not, a successful treatment program includes a psychological component to understand the reasons for use (eg trauma, coping strategies etc), how best to deal with triggers, and to create an identity where sobriety exists.

It is worth noting that for some people, sobriety and abstinence are not one in the same. Sobriety can mean different things for different people and different addictions. When it comes to substances, most people view abstinence as the definition of sobriety. Conversely, we would never expect someone to be abstinent if they have a food addiction. Instead, we would encourage a healthy relationship with food. The same can be accomplished with other addictions.

There are some who also differentiate between addiction and dependency. They believe that dependence is a component of addiction, and not the same as addiction. To them, dependence is the increased physical tolerance of legally acquired medications. Conversely, addiction is seen as the physical tolerance coupled with a psychological dependence. This is turn leads to behavioural symptoms such as lying and stealing.

The mediator should explore this topic with the parties as even those in the same family dealing with the same issue may have a different definition or desired outcome. Understanding this information will also help the mediator manage the situation if the addiction issue is raised during the joint mediation session.

NARRATIVE:

While processing the topic of addiction with a client, they became very withdrawn. They informed me that they once had an addiction to opiates. They were prescribed opiates following a surgery, and over time, they became dependent. To stop taking the opiates, they then engaged in a medically supervised opiate cessation program.

While this person was actively using opiates, they only used what was prescribed by a doctor. They never stole to get drugs. They never lied to get drugs. They never got drugs off the street. They also actively participated in a medically supervised program to stop using opiates. In spite of those facts, the client carried intense shame over the fact that they were "addicted" to opiates. This was a situation when the Addiction vs. Dependency conversation would have been beneficial.

SUPPORT PERSON:

Often during the intake process, people will ask to bring a support person to the joint mediation session. Whether or not a participant brings a support person is their choice. None of the other participants have the ability to deny a support person. They do however, have the ability to say they will not sit in the same room as the support person. They may also choose not to participate at all if a certain support person is present.

If a participant indicates that they would like to bring a support person, the mediator should discuss this with the client. It is important to process why the participant feels it is necessary to bring a support person, and there should also be discussion as to how they think the other parties will react. The mediator needs to ensure that all participants know that if they wish to bring a support person to the joint mediation session, they need to inform the mediator of this beforehand.

The mediator has an obligation to inform the other parties that someone is bringing a support person, and who the support person will be. The mediator should then also ask the other parties if they would like to bring a support person. It can be problematic if someone arrives at the joint mediation session with a support person, and nobody knew about it ahead of time.

SURPRISES = DRAMA

As mentioned, the choice of support person is that of the individual participant. It may be a family member, a friend, or even their lawyer. The role of the support person is very specific, and should be reviewed with the participant and support person before the joint mediation session. Regardless of the support person's connection with the participant, they are attending the mediation as support. They are not the one engaged in the negotiation, and they are not a decision maker. This is especially important to cover with the parties and their supports if everyone is to be in the same room for the joint mediation session.

This also requires special attention when lawyers are present. When a client retains a lawyer, the lawyer plays an incredibly important role in the mediation process. Their role is to provide their clients with legal advice and information, and to advocate for their client's best interests. They want to ensure that their client gets a fair deal and also, they want to ensure that their client does not agree to anything counterintuitive to their goals.

Some lawyers advocate more strongly than others. During mediation sessions, this may lead to the lawyers dominating the conversation. Mediators need to do their best to ensure that decisions are being made by the clients; not the lawyers. They also need to ensure that dominant personalities and legal knowledge do not create additional power imbalances.

SOURCE OF INCOME:

During the intake process, it is helpful to ask clients about their source of income. The amount is not of importance, but understanding where the income comes from can be. Many clients that we work with are connected with subsidized income programs such as Social Assistance (eg Ontario Works) and Disability Support Programs (eg ODSP - Ontario Disability Support Program).

If a person is "on Disability," it is useful to ask follow-up questions as to why they are receiving assistance. Reasons may include, but are not limited to:
- intellectual disabilities
- physical disabilities
- literacy challenges
- mental health challenges

By understanding more about the person's need for assistance, the mediator is better equipped to design a mediation process that fits the clients. This may include, but is not limited to:
- modifying the length of joint mediation sessions
- reading documents to clients instead of having them read documents themselves
- providing written information to clients in advance of future meetings
- encouraging a support person

Another benefit to asking about a person's income source relates to scheduling. By having a sense of the person's income source, the mediator has a better understanding of the client's schedule. For example, people on Social Assistance or Disability are often not working. As a result, they are likely to have more flexibility during the day to attend appointments. People that work Monday to Friday 9-5 are likely to require evening appointments. And those who are self-employed are likely to have very dynamic schedules.

SCHEDULING:

Ask clients if there are preferred days or times to meet for a joint mediation session if the mediation moves forward. This will save time when scheduling the joint session. If the mediator has a sense of the clients' availability, they can start from there when looking at their own calendars. This will avoid multiple emails, phone calls etc to schedule appointments. If the determination is to do a shuttle mediation, ensure that clients are scheduled for different arrival times.

TERMINATION/ BOUNDARIES:

At the end of the intake appointment, I ask clients if they have any questions for me. I also ask if there is anything I need to know that we had not gone over in the intake appointment. As mentioned previous, there is no way to cover everything; even with our questionnaire templates. Asking the clients if they have anything additional to share gives them permission to have some free narrative on anything they feel is important.

I also use this as a means of setting some boundaries. At the beginning of the intake appointment, I give the clients my business card. At the end, I remind them that they have my contact information if they think of anything important that they forgot to share in the intake appointment.

At this point, I let them know that the phone number on my business card is a cellular phone. I give the clients permission to text, but remind them to put their name on the text. I inform them that I will use text messaging to schedule appointments only, and I will not use text messaging to discuss case details or process. I remind clients that if they feel the need to contact me to report on the actions of the other party, I will reply that they need to consult with their lawyer or their worker. My role is not to have those discussions outside of the mediation meetings with the clients, and this re-establishes my role as the mediator; not as a worker or other service provider.

Clients often ask if there is anything that they need to bring to the joint mediation session. Prior to clients leaving their intake appointment, I give them a second business card. On the front is my business logo, and on the back are some joint mediation session prep tips. They are:

- consult with a lawyer about your rights & responsibilities
- arrange your own transportation to and from the appointment (do NOT travel with the other party)
- bring any existing court order(s)
- bring variances to any no-contact/ restraining orders
- bring a list of topics to discuss
- do NOT bring children
- if bringing a support person, you must inform the mediator BEFORE the joint mediation session so the mediator may inform the other party
- come prepared to work with the other party; not against them

Mediation caseloads can be very high at times. During those times, it may take more than a reasonable amount of time to get back to clients. I suggest to clients that if they have not heard back from me within two weeks, they should follow up, and ask for an update. This gives clients permission to follow up, and empowers them to be part of the process; not just a passenger.

I also provide clients with a copy of the Agreement To Mediate to be signed at the beginning of the Joint Mediation Session. I ask them to review the document prior to the joint mediation session, and to contact me before the mediation if they have any questions.

NARRATIVE:

During a mediation intake appointment, you will see and hear some outrageous things. It is important to remain calm and non-reactive during these times and if necessary, debrief with a colleague after. If you react to the information, it will send a message to the client. If one person is disclosing information about a different person, your reaction of disapproval may create a perceived bias for the client. They may feel they've won you over, or that you are not sympathetic to their concerns. If you have an opinion on their information and it is beneficial to share it, do so in a diplomatic fashion. Also, if you see something unnerving in an appointment, filter your response.

An example of something you may hear during an intake appointment may revolve around sex and sexuality. As mentioned earlier, I enquire about addictions during intake appointments. The initial response was "No," because when we think of addictions, we often focus on drugs and alcohol. I then listed several types of addiction including pornography. The client then disclosed that pornography was the final straw for her in the relationship.

She had done a search of the family computer's browser history, and found upsetting pornography which included bestiality. It was very important for me to remain non-reactive during that time. As the partner of someone who looked at those images, she was likely having her own reactions such as confusion, self-doubt, and possibly trauma. Had I reacted negatively, it may no longer have felt like a safe environment for her to share her thoughts and feelings. There is also the possibility that she would have reported back to the former partner that "the mediator thought X about your bestiality pictures." The other side may then feel there is little chance for a balanced mediation at that point. As a result, I would have been left unable to help the family.

NARRATIVE:

Another example of filtered reactions was during an FGDM intake appointment. I was working with a parent who had intellectual delays, and the purpose of the process was long-term placement of the child. During the intake appointment at the dining room table (*Reminder*: FGDM intakes are different than Mediation intakes), the client picked their toenail, and then started eating it. Inside, I was appalled, but I had to remain straight-faced. Reacting negatively would have had significant negative consequences on the meeting, and the ability to move forward in the process.

Although these are not everyday experiences, they do happen. No two days are alike, and you need to be prepared for anything. Being reactive could have significant consequences for the family with whom you are working, and for your professional reputation.

WORKER

The worker's intake appointment is very similar to a family member's intake appointment. In the spirit of maintaining neutrality and treating everyone as equals, the worker also signs the confidentiality agreement. This also makes workers aware of the experience that family members go through during the intake process. Although I do not read the Confidentiality Agreement to workers, some time is still spent on explaining what each paragraph means. It is also important during their intake to remind the worker that they are not permitted to take any notes on the day of the joint mediation session. An example of a Worker Intake Form can be seen in *Appendix E*.

OCL:

The mediator should ask the worker if OCL has been notified of the mediation referral. It is not uncommon for workers to respond with "It's not in court." Remind the workers that the OCL needs to be informed of every case that is referred to mediation, using the prescribed Notice of ADR form. If the referral has been submitted, the mediator should enquire as to whether or not the OCL has made a decision with respect to their involvement. It is acceptable for the mediator to reach out to the OCL directly.

If a lawyer is already involved to represent the child, the mediator needs to ensure that the worker has informed the lawyer of the mediation referral.

INTERVIEW CHILDREN:

Spend some time with the worker discussing how the children are doing, and how they are impacted by the situation requiring CAS intervention. The worker will have valuable insight into the well-being of the children, and also have suggestions on how to engage the child in an interview. Workers are often actively engaged with service providers connected with the children, and are often able to help determine if there is a benefit to meeting with the children as part of the mediation process.

HISTORY:

When meeting with the worker, the mediator needs to ask questions as to when the CAS file opened, reason for service, and any changes since the file opened. The mediator must also explore any incidents of domestic violence (physical, emotional and/ or verbal), intimidation, and/ or control. CAS will also often have information related to a participants' substance use and mental health. The mediator should also ask if the worker has any concerns with the idea of the parties being in the room together, or with being in the same room themselves with the family members.

SUPPORT PERSON:

In some communities, CAS Supervisors will join the worker for the intake appointment. This is agency-specific, and not mandatory for the mediation process. It is the choice of the CAS, and should not be directed by the mediator or the TPA. Much like a family member, the CAS is a party to the mediation. It is acceptable for a family member to bring a support person to their intake appointment, so it is also acceptable for a worker to have their Supervisor participate in the CAS intake appointment. The benefit to a supervisor being present for the intake appointment is that they will have a first-hand understanding of the discussions with respect to history, worries, strengths, and mediation goals. A shortcoming is there is an additional person with whom schedules have to be coordinated.

The mediator should spend some time with the worker to explain the support person concept for the joint mediation session(s). As with family members, workers may also have feelings about a family member's choice in support person. The choice however, is the individual participant's. In general, CAS supervisors and/ or CAS lawyers do not attend the group mediation session unless the family members are bringing their lawyers. There is a perceived power imbalance towards CAS by virtue of their authority, and having multiple CAS staff present during a joint mediation session may be very intimidating to family members.

SCHEDULING:

Explore scheduling with the worker. Most CAS agencies have standard hours of operation from 8:30am to 4:30pm or 9am to 5pm Monday to Friday. Although there is always After-Hours coverage, the majority of CAS staff work during the day. Although many of our families are not working, there are many that are working; some of them "working poor." If they take time off work, some clients run the risk of losing their job. The mediator needs to have discussions with the worker as to whether or not the worker is available for evening appointments and/ or weekend appointments. The mediator should also be open to this concept if they are going to adequately service the child welfare population.

Bottom Lines:

The mediator should strongly recommend that the worker have a case consultation/ supervision with their supervisor prior to the joint mediation session(s). During that supervision, the worker and supervisor should brainstorm potential outcomes that may be suggested by the family members during the mediation. That way, the worker will be in a better position to make decisions during the mediation without the need for additional consultation with their supervisor.

The mediator should also encourage the worker to have conversations with the family members prior to the group mediation session(s). The worker should explain to families if there are certain issues that are not open for discussion. An example of this may be placement of the children. The CAS may have a position that a child will not be returned to a parent's care, and the mediation is to discuss access. The parent needs to be aware of this ahead of time, so they are not disappointed if they feel the mediation is to discuss reintegration.

If possible and the family members are comfortable with the idea, they too should inform the other parties if there are topics not open for discussion. Although it may narrow the mediation subject matter, it may also prevent an unnecessary waste of everyone's time.

NARRATIVE:

The child had been removed the mother's care by CAS, and then placed with the paternal grandparents. Although Dad was not involved on a regular basis, he was somewhat involved. Also, he supported the placement with the grandparents.

As time went on, the mother continued to struggle with the issues that led to the child being apprehended, and the CAS position was that the child remain with the grandparents. As a result, a referral was made for CP Med to discuss what the mother's ongoing contact with the child would look like.

I explored the background and the issues with each of the parties during their intake appointments. I also explored what each party wanted out of the mediation (ie their goals). CAS was clear that they "wanted" the child to remain with the paternal grandparents. Unfortunately, I was not clear with CAS that if their position was non-negotiable, they needed to inform the mother before the joint mediation session.

When we arrived at the joint mediation session, the mother was ill-prepared. She was there to talk about reintegration, and reintegration only. She was very clear that she was not there to talk about access. Her position was that the child was to be returned to her care within two weeks, and it was non-negotiable.

As a result, the joint mediation session failed miserably, and quickly. The mother had taken a day off work, and so had the grandparents. Also, the grandparents had driven over an hour one-way for the meeting. Ultimately, the case went to trial and in the end, it was a complete waste of time, and Ministry resources.

SAFE TERMINATION

Not all mediations go forward, and there are many reasons why this is the case. Ultimately, it is up to the mediator's discretion if they believe that they can facilitate a process that is beneficial and safe. If not, they have an obligation to screen the case out. Informing the clients that mediation is not moving forward may be done differently by different mediators, but there is an obligation to do so in a safe way. Remember, although the final decision to screen out comes later, safe termination begins during the intake introductions.

When a decision is made to terminate the mediation, best practice is to phone the parties to inform them. It is also beneficial to send a

Closing Letter to all of the parties indicating that the mediation is not moving forward. In the Closing Letter, indicate that the mediation is not moving forward, and that the reasons cannot be disclosed. A suggestion is to also include a statement that says the decision is not a reflection on any one person. An example can be found in *Appendix F*.

If the case has been screened out and there is a more suitable process than mediation, it is ok to inform the parties of the other process. Be certain to provide all of the parties with the same information, so that there are no misunderstandings. Depending on the reasons and the mediator's comfort level, it may also be possible to indicate why the other process may be more suitable. Use discretion however, as this may put people at risk. What the mediator says during these conversations is not always what the clients hear.

Some clients are happy that their file has been screened out of mediation, and others are disappointed. The mediator may receive inquiries as to why the mediation is not moving forward and sometimes, clients will become very persistent in their requests for mediation to move ahead. The mediator must remain careful about the information they provide. Once they have made a decision to terminate the mediation, barring any new information, the mediation should be terminated. When in doubt, the mediator needs to follow their gut instincts about the people and the case.

Some examples of why CP Med may not move forward include, but are not limited to:
- a serious incident recently occurred & one or more of the parties is too emotional/ upset to carry on a useful conversation, or make important decisions
- you strongly suspect that one of more of the parties intends to use the mediation to escalate the dispute (threaten, gather information for personal reasons or to share with the court)

- one party seems incapable of listening to anything you say
- you feel there is a more suitable process
- one of the parties is unwilling to participate

In my experience, the most common reason a CP Med does not move forward is because of unwillingness of a party to participate. Although a client may tell you outright that they are not interested in mediation, more often than not, their lack of intent is demonstrated through their actions. It is very common for clients not to return phone calls and text messages, and simply avoid the mediator. There are also situations when they do not show up for scheduled mediation appointments. Best practice is to attempt to follow up with the client but if you are not successful after two or three attempts, the client is sending a very clear message. Close the file!

VOICE OF THE CHILD

The United Nations Convention on the Rights of the Child and the CYFSA define a child as any person under the age of eighteen (18). In the past, the CFSA defined a child as a person under the age of sixteen (16) unless there was a court finding of a child in need of protection. In 2018 however, the CYFSA raised the age of eligibility to include those under the age of eighteen (18). Although the age of protection increased to eighteen (18), children aged sixteen (16) and seventeen (17) are entitled to refuse services offered by CAS.

KATELYNN'S PRINCIPLE

Many of the changes from the CFSA to the CYFSA revolve around Katelynn's Principle. Katelynn's Principle is a private member's bill (Bill 57), and it is based on recommendations from the Coroner's Inquest after Katelynn Sampson's death. Seven year old Katelynn died in 2008. The inquest concluded in April 2016 with 173 recommendations for Child Welfare, Law Enforcement, and Educators. Her death was ruled a homicide by her caregivers as a result of "complications from multiple blunt force injuries."

Katelynn's Principle is to be applied when making decisions that affect a child. The following are collectively known as Katelynn's Principle:

1. The child must be at the centre of the decision.
2. The child is an individual with rights. The child must always be seen, the child's voice must be heard, and the child must be listened to and respected.
3. The child's heritage must be taken into consideration and respected. Attention must be paid to the broad and diverse

communities the child identifies with, including communities defined by matters such as race, ethnicity, religion, language, and sexual orientation.
4. Actions must be taken to ensure that a child who is capable of forming their own views is able to express those views freely and safely about matters affecting them.
5. The child's views must be given due weight in accordance with the child's age and maturity.
6. In accordance with the child's age and maturity, the child must be given the opportunity to participate before any decisions affecting the child are made, whether the participation is direct or through a support person or representative.
7. In accordance with the child's age and maturity, the child must be engaged through honest and respectful dialogue about how and why decisions affecting them are made.
8. Every person who provides services to children or services affecting children is a child advocate. Advocacy may be a child's lifeline and it must occur from the point of first contact and on a continuous basis thereafter.

As mentioned earlier, there has been a shift in mediation in recent years to include the voice of the child. Yet, there are still some who feel meeting with the child only serves to bring the child further into the conflict. Truth be told however, children are often already very much involved in the situation as a direct result of the actions (or inaction) of adults. When looking at the best interests of a child, it is helpful to have an understanding of the child's views and experiences. Furthermore, Katelynn's Principle implores us to hear the child's voice, and this allows for empowerment of the child.

Although Katelynn's Principle is not legislated as of yet, there are elements of it included in the CYFSA. For example, Section 3 of the CYFSA is with respect to the rights of children, and young people receiving services under the CYFSA. Section 3 states:

Every child and young person receiving services under this Act has the following rights:

1. *To express their own views freely and safely about matters that affect them.*
2. *To be engaged through an honest and respectful dialogue about how and why decisions affecting them are made and to have their views given due weight, in accordance with their age and maturity.*
3. *To be consulted on the nature of the services provided or to be provided to them, to participate in decisions about the services provided or to be provided to them and to be advised of the decisions made in respect of those services.*
4. *To raise concerns or recommend changes with respect to the services provided or to be provided to them without interference or fear of coercion, discrimination or reprisal and to receive a response to their concerns or recommended changes.*
5. *To be informed, in language suitable to their understanding, of their rights under this Part.*
6. *To be informed, in language suitable to their understanding, of the existence and role of the Provincial Advocate for Children and Youth and of how the Provincial Advocate for Children and Youth may be contacted.*

It should be stated that Section 3 of the CYFSA does not mandate the mediator to meet with the children. It is mandating that the voice of the child be heard. Depending on the situation, that voice may be heard through an OCL, the Worker, or the mediator. It is important for the mediator to assess the method that they believe to be the most useful on a case-by-case basis.

The voice of the child can sometimes be a difficult conversation to have with adults. Many adults question the reasons why the mediator wishes to speak with a child. Given the family is involved with CAS, there may be some fear as to what the mediator will discuss with the child but also, the parent may be trying to shelter the child. Section 3 of the CYFSA makes the conversation a bit easier to have, but it is beneficial to help parents understand the function and necessity of the information gathering.

Dr Michael Saini, Chair of Law and Social Work at University of Toronto describes the decision-making process as a pizza. Each participant is a piece of the pizza; the parents, OCL, Protection Worker, Mediator, & child. All of these pieces are necessary to facilitate a comprehensive process, and to make agreements that fit the family. Without the voice of the child, there is a key piece missing. Dr Saini reminds us that if you ordered a pizza, you would not accept the delivery if it was missing a piece. Yet, we are prepared to make lasting arrangements for children without taking their voice into consideration.

NOTHING ABOUT ME WITHOUT ME
- FGC Ontario Provincial Resource -

Prior to making a determination as to whether or not to meet with a child, the mediator needs to have completed intakes with all of the adult parties, and determined that the case is suitable for mediation. The mediator must assess whether there is benefit to meeting with the child or if it will do more harm. Many children involved in the child welfare system have been interviewed many times by many different people. The mediator needs to be sensitive to that fact, and not over-interview the child.

DO NO HARM

The mediator should not meet with children unless they have completed training on how to appropriately interview children, and are comfortable with the interview process. Interviewing a seven year old is very different than interviewing a fifteen (15) year old, and the mediator must know how to interact with the child in an age-appropriate manner. If you are not comfortable interviewing children or you are not adequately trained to do so, another option is to hire a clinician with that skill set. Ensure that clinician also understands the role of the child's voice in the mediation process.

The mediator's goal of meeting with the child is to get a sense of who is in the child's life, and how they are managing with the current situation. It is imperative that the mediator not conduct a "Safety Interview" in the same manner as a CAS worker. Occasionally however, a disclosure does happen. If this occurs, the mediator needs to know how to manage that situation, and do the least possible harm to the child and to any possible investigation after the fact.

The mediator should only meet with the children if there is a perceived benefit to meeting with them. Meeting with children just for the sake of meeting with them serves no purpose other than financial gain for the mediator. If the mediator feels they are missing valuable information or the parents' understanding of the child's wishes are grossly different, there is merit to meeting with the child. It is also helpful at the joint mediation session if the mediator is able to reference the child with first-hand knowledge, and describe certain personality traits of the child. This helps clients to focus on why they are in mediation; for the best interests of the child.

CREATIVITY

Children are incredibly creative, and wise. The saying *Out of the mouths of babes* implies that children speak the truth and have incredible wisdom. Oftentimes, children will come up with solutions that adults could not create. This may be a result of the innocence of youth and the fact that as we age, we often become more confined and structured in our thinking. Children have not learned limitations to their creative thought processes, and are not yet limited by social norms. They speak from a perspective of honesty and emotion. They say and do things simply because it feels right. It is not because of social convention or because it is what they have been told to say, think, draw, etc.

> **EVERY CHILD IS AN ARTIST.
> THE PROBLEM IS HOW TO REMAIN AN ARTIST
> ONCE WE GROW UP.**
> *- Pablo Picasso -*

In mediation, we are not stuck with the confines and restrictions of the legal system. We are able to be creative in ways that lawyers and judges cannot entertain in a court system. As a result, clients are able to develop a plan that fits their situation, as opposed to forcing their family to fit the legal model. This creates better outcomes for families and in particular, for children. Utilizing the creativity of children can sometimes bring a unique perspective to the room, and help create better outcomes for families.

NARRATIVE:

My youngest son had been potty trained during the day for well over a year, yet he still struggled to remain dry at night. He would frequently wake up with a wet diaper and many times, his pajamas and bedding would also be wet. My wife and I were becoming increasingly frustrated by the situation, especially as my son got older.

We tried different strategies, but nothing seemed to be very effective. Our closest brush with success was a specific reward if he was able to wake up dry for seven nights in a row. On more than one occasion, he made it to six nights. Unfortunately, he would be wet on morning seven.

One morning while getting my youngest dressed, my then six year old made a suggestion. His suggestion was to make a chart. My youngest child would get points for a dry diaper, and lose points for a wet diaper. When my youngest reached a target number, he would get a prize. I asked my oldest to share his idea with my wife/ his mother, and her and I agreed to try the plan. My youngest also thought this was a good idea.

Within about two and a half weeks, he had earned his prize. Over the next two months, there were only two wet diapers in the morning. Shortly after that, we transitioned to no overnight diapers, and wet beds became few and far between. So by listening to the unfiltered creativity of a child, we were able to find a realistic and successful solution.

YOU ARE ONLY LIMITED BY YOUR IMAGINATION

OCL

If a lawyer has been appointed by the OCL to represent the child in the CP Med process, the child's lawyer then becomes the mediator's gatekeeper to the child. The lawyer will decide if the mediator meets with the child. Also, it is the lawyer's role to inform the child about the process, and what the process looks like.

The lawyer will also decide in consultation with their client, in what capacity the child will participate in the mediation. If the child is young, it is unlikely that they will attend the joint mediation session. If the child is older however, they may attend. Some ways in which children can actively participate in the joint mediation sessions include but are not limited to:
- child not physically present but their lawyer attends
- in the same room (with lawyer present)
- in a different room (with their lawyer)
- in a different room (lawyer with the adults and providing child with updates)

The lawyer and mediator together will determine the best method of sharing the child's views and preferences with the adults. Ways in which the child's lawyer may share the child's views and preferences include but are not limited to:
- to the group at the beginning of the joint mediation session
- to the group throughout the joint mediation session
- to each adult privately with the mediator present
- to each parent privately with the child and mediator present

If an OCL is appointed and/ or the Eligibility Spectrum Code is a 4-2 (Parent-Child Conflict), the child is an equal party to the mediation; much the same way the child would be an equal in the eyes of the court if an OCL was appointed. That means that they have just as much ability to say 'Yes' or 'No' to anything in the mediation, and their agreement is necessary for an item to be included in the Memorandum of Understanding. That said, OCL lawyers often encourage the parents to take ownership of child-related decisions in an effort to take pressure off of the children. For example, parents may reach an agreement with respect to the child's schedule and the child may not be in complete agreement. Barring any significant worries, the lawyer is likely to support the parents' agreement as it is in the best interests of their client.

As with the adults, the child's interview is confidential. The mediator needs to explain this to the child at the beginning of the meeting. Although the mediator meets with the child privately (unless OCL is assigned and present), it is helpful to have the conversation of confidentiality with the parent present. It takes the pressure off the child if an adult asks later what they spoke about, and the child does not want to share. At the end of the child's interview, the mediator should ask the child's permission to share specific content (eg views and preferences) that may be useful in the joint mediation session. If the child does not consent, the information remains confidential.

NARRATIVE:

There are instances when mediators have to think outside the box, and look at the bigger picture. No more was this more apparent than with the *Kenneth* family. At the time of mediation, the parents had been separated for approximately nine years, yet remained embroiled in considerable conflict.

The mother was in her late forties, lived in a major city, and had been the victim of significant domestic violence, both by the father of the child, and by her most recent partner. Her recent partner was also verbally abusive to the children. Mum had a family court order granting her Sole Custody and Primary Residence of the child.
The father was in his late thirties and lived in a small town approximately two hours away from the city. Approximately ten years ago, he suffered a psychotic break as a result of drug use. He had since remarried, and had two young children. In family court,

Dad was granted alternate weekend parenting time with his child, *Carson*.

Carson was a thirteen year old boy. He was well-spoken, and had a gentle demeanor. There were no negative reports from school, and he was described as "kind and sweet" by the worker. He also had an adult brother who lived with him at his mother's. He would travel alone on the train to visit with Dad. *Carson* described how Mum was previously in an abusive relationship and "I saw it all." He would become particularly upset with Mum when she would compare Dad to the abusive ex-partner.

It was very clear that a traditional mediated agreement was unlikely with the involved parties. Through consultation with *Carson's* lawyer (appointed by the OCL) and the worker, a decision was made to help facilitate an information-sharing appointment for the parents. Given the personalities of the parents, we felt the best possible outcome would be for the parents to hear about *Carson's* feelings.

We began the "mediation" in the same room to establish some ground rules for the day. There was information gathered and shared that was important for everyone to hear at once. We then separated the parents.

With *Carson* present, his lawyer shared his thoughts and feelings with each parent privately. I was aware of this information ahead of time, as I had met with *Carson* and his lawyer for a confidential intake and again, immediately before the mediation began. Dad was very accepting of the information but unfortunately, Mum was explosive. We expected that Mum would have difficulties hearing the information, but felt the reward for *Carson* outweighed the risk.

As a result of our approach, the child was able to share his feelings around the parents' ongoing conflict. Although Mum was not accepting of her role in the conflict, Dad was accepting. Moving forward, he made efforts to engage less in conflict with Mum as he saw that as more beneficial to his child.

Although not a traditional mediation, the voice of the child was extremely important in this case. *Carson* was given an opportunity to express his thoughts and feelings in a safe place and in a safe way. This would create a platform for him to express himself in the future but also, it gave him an opportunity to see who was truly listening to him and looking out for his best interests. I later found out that very soon after the joint mediation session, *Carson* went to live with his father and did quite well in his care.

JOINT MEDIATION SESSION(S)

Love is better than anger. Hope is better than fear. Optimism is better than despair. So let us be loving, hopeful, and optimistic, and we'll change the world.
- Jack Layton

WHO IS PRESENT?

In CP Med, an agent from CAS must be present for the joint mediation session(s). CAS has an interest in the outcome, and is considered one of the parties. Furthermore, CAS will be responsible for monitoring how the agreement is carried out, as well as assisting with the implementation of the agreement. If the CAS does not have an interest in the outcome and are not present for the joint mediation session, it is no longer a CP Med. It becomes a Family Mediation, and Family Mediation is not funded by MCYS.

If a lawyer has been appointed to represent the child in the mediation process, the lawyer must also be present for the joint mediation sessions. This is especially important if the matter is before the court, and the parties intend on making the agreement into a court order.

FORMAT

The mediator needs to be early for the joint mediation session to make sure that the rooms are ready to accommodate the parties upon their arrival. This will prevent any of the parties from spending an excessive amount of time in the waiting area. If the mediator is planning to hold a shuttle mediation, the parties should be given varying arrival times to avoid any client contact in the parking lot, waiting room etc.

Once the parties are in the room for the joint mediation session, the mediator will establish some housekeeping items. If there have been any no-contact conditions among the parties, the joint mediation session should only be occurring if there has been a variance of some sort. The mediator should let the parties know of this variance at the outset, as one or more of the parties may be very nervous about that issue.

Remind the parties that all communication up until that point in time is confidential, and cannot be shared. The mediator is essentially starting with a clean slate. Inform the parties that once the Agreement To Mediate (ATM) is signed, all communication is for the group; even if the parties are in separate rooms. If the parties wish to have a confidential conversation (caucus) with the mediator after the ATM is signed, the party must inform the mediator that the content is confidential.

It is also a good time to remind clients that the focus is on the future. What has happened up until that point in time is done, and in the past. It cannot be changed. Although the mediator may need to discuss the past somewhat, the past cannot dominate the session. The focus needs to be on shifting to the future, and in doing things differently.

FOCUS ON FORWARD

NARRATIVE:

I use the phrase "Focus On Forward" at the beginning of almost all of my joint mediation sessions. To help clients understand the importance of looking to the future, I describe a race. I inform them that as a group, we are going to run from one end of the parking lot to the other. Half of the group will run while looking ahead to the finish line. The other half of the group will run towards the finish line, but while looking behind them the whole time.

I rhetorically ask them who will get to the finish line first. Obviously, it will be the people running forwards, and looking to the finish. They are focussed on the goal, the future, and doing things differently. I then remind clients that the people always looking to the past will not likely make it to the finish line, and if they do, they will take longer and have an increased chance of injury.

Without Prejudice Settlement Discussions

Spend some time explaining that the joint mediation sessions are without prejudice settlement discussions. That is to say that the content of the meetings will not be used against anyone, people have the ability to change their minds, and the ultimate goal is to make progress towards an agreement. This is a good opportunity to remind all of the parties that the mediator is the only person who may take notes. Workers may enter a casenote indicating that they attended mediation on that date and who was present but in reality, they do not even need to document that. The only documentation that comes out of the joint mediation session is the Memorandum of Understanding (MOU).

AGREEMENT TO MEDIATE

Policy Directive CW 005-06 is very clear that an Agreement to Mediate (ATM) *should* be used in the CP Med process. The ATM specifically needs to outline the confidentiality provisions of the

CP Med process contained in the Regulation. These provisions need to be clearly explained to all of the parties at the beginning of the joint mediation session or earlier, so that the parties are able to make informed decisions about their participation.

The Policy Directive further notes that having a written ATM may act as a disincentive for some people. This would likely apply to individuals with literacy issues. If the parties do not sign a written ATM, the mediator must ensure that the confidentiality provisions are reviewed with the parties, understood, and agreed to by the parties. In the event that a written ATM is not signed by the participants, the Policy Directive states that the worker MUST document the reasons in the family's file.

In an effort to streamline the process and avoid miscommunication, it is beneficial to read the ATM to all of the parties at the beginning of the joint mediation. It will save time as everyone hears the content at once instead of waiting for each participant to read the document. Also, it can avoid having people feeling marginalized if they have literacy challenges. It is helpful to circulate a copy of the ATM, so participants can follow along while the mediator is reading the ATM. Best practice is that the mediator explain each part of the ATM clearly to all of the parties, and also offer the parties a copy of the signed ATM. That way, participants may further review the document at a later date.

An example of a standard ATM can be found in *Appendix G*.

NARRATIVE:

Relatively early in my CP Med career, I ran into an obstacle with respect to the ATM. In attendance for the mediation were four family members, the Protection Worker, three lawyers and myself. Prior to the joint mediation session, I had completed confidential intake appointments with all of the parties, and had discussions with their lawyers. I had previously held joint mediation sessions with two of the lawyers present on other files, so they were very familiar with me and the process. It was my first time with one lawyer in particular attending a joint mediation session. In an effort to streamline the day, I provided the lawyer with a copy of the ATM prior to beginning the joint mediation session. The lawyer had no questions.

When the joint mediation session began, I reviewed the ATM with the group. In doing so, I clarified that no parties or their lawyers were to take any notes. The lawyer in question challenged this as it had not been clearly noted in the ATM. Their position was that to fully advocate for their client, they needed to take notes. I pushed back that note-taking was not permissible, but the lawyer indicated that the only way mediation could continue is if they were permitted to take notes.

The other two lawyers in the room stated that they had never been told in the past that they couldn't take notes in a CP Med, but that they were not going to take notes during the process. This was particularly confusing for me, because both lawyers had participated in mediation with me in the past. All of the parties agreed to allow the lawyer to take notes and as a result, the joint mediation session occurred.

Although I put it back to the parties to decide on this issue, it was a breach of one of the fundamental ideals of the CP Med process; it is a closed process. There was no way to guarantee that information from the session and outside of the MOU would not be used aas evidence in court. Although the other lawyers would likely protest and the information would not be admissible, it is impossible to un-hear something. In hindsight, I should have spent more time preparing the lawyer, and also not preceded with the mediation if the lawyer insisted on note-taking.

As a result of this experience, I have added the following to my ATM's:

> *No parties, including their lawyers, shall take any notes or recordings of any joint mediation session(s). The only exception to this rule is with respect to a lawyer representing a child when the child is not in attendance for the joint mediation session(s). Notes taken by a child's lawyer shall only contain a list of agreements reached in principle.*

The OCL exception is a result of the child-client not be present for the joint mediation session, and the lawyer's responsibility to report back to their client.

NARRATIVE:

Both of the parents had lawyers, and requested that their lawyers attend as their support person for the mediation. I had worked with Lawyer1 several times, and had an excellent rapport with that lawyer. Lawyer2 was relatively new to the local Bar, and I had never worked with them directly. Further, Lawyer2 had a reputation in the community as being a very confrontational lawyer, with a strong personality. To top it off, Lawyer2 had never been involved in a CP Med before.

In an effort to prevent a repeat of the roadblock in the previous Narrative, I sent the lawyers and the worker a copy of the Agreement To Mediation approximately one week before the joint mediation session. I also asked that the lawyers review the ATM with their clients before the joint mediation session. These parents were not high-functioning adults, and my hope was that time would not be wasted at the beginning of the joint mediation session explaining the ATM. Unfortunately, that was not the case.

Prior to the joint mediation session, Lawyer1 questioned the wording of the following confidentiality provision:

The terms of an agreement, memorandum of understanding or plan arising from the mediation may be shared with the court, and all lawyers, including lawyers for the child(ren) where applicable.

Lawyer1's concern was that the mediator may be filing the MOU with the court. I clarified that this was not accurate, but Lawyer1 also had concerns that consent should be required prior to the parties filing the MOU with the court. Their worry was that if a party files the MOU and another party changes their mind on any of the points, it may become prejudicial.

Lawyer2 also agreed with this point, but appeared more concerned with the wording "or plan" in the paragraph. In spite of my best efforts, Lawyer2 did not seem to accept that "The Plan" referred to the document prepared with respect to Family Group Conferencing/ Family Group Decision-Making.

Both lawyers continued to put pressure on me with respect to the wording of "my" ATM. So, I showed them the ATM from a different service provider. The wording of that paragraph was identical. Still, they didn't agree. So, I showed them the (identical) wording from the CFSA Regulation 496/ 06. Surprisingly, they still balked.

I was left with a very difficult decision. I could modify the wording to say "except on consent of the parties" and remove "or plan" from the ATM, or I could close my process. Although making the amendments seems like an easy out, it was not the right decision. Changing the document would have compromised my integrity on principle and further, I would no longer be following the language prescribed by the MCYS. I am uncertain what the ramifications would be of this, so I stayed true to the wording.

In the end, the lawyers agreed to proceed with mediation. Prior to ending the first joint mediation session, I spent extra time reviewing the agreements reached in principle, and even reviewed the wording I use for specific outcomes.

The lesson is that if you chose to use specific language in your documentation, you need to ensure that the language fits with the process. You also need to ensure that if there is backlash, you have sound reasons for using the language that you use.

Background Information

After the parties sign the ATM, the mediator needs to acquire some background information. This is valuable information to include at the beginning of the MOU. It may also help to begin some of the conversations in the joint mediation session. Some background information to collect includes, but is not limited to:

- the children's names and dates of birth
- if children are First Nations, Inuit, or Métis and if so, what Band
- if the matter is before the court and if so, which court (Family Court or CAS court), and when it returns to court
- if the parties have retained lawyers and if so, the names of their lawyers
- Date of Marriage (if applicable) and Date of Separation (if applicable)
- when the CAS file opened
- child's doctor, dentist, religious affiliation, school

First and foremost, the mediator needs to have the correct spelling of the names of the children, and their dates of birth. The mediator should also differentiate if there are other children connected to the file, but not a subject of the mediation. That is, clients may have children with other partners with whom they are not in mediation.

If the parties have not retained a lawyer, the mediator should list whether or not the parties have sought out Independent Legal Advice. For any judge and/ or lawyer reviewing the MOU at a later date, it will prompt them to ask questions as to whether or not the party fully understands the MOU. It also highlights that the mediator asked the parties if they had received ILA and if they had not, the mediator likely encouraged them to seek out ILA.

If the mediation referral is with respect to adult conflict or custody and access, knowing the date of marriage and date of separation may help the mediator to explore how long the conflict has been going on. It may also provide some options to explore times when the family was not engaged in the same level of conflict.

If the matter is before the courts, the judge is likely to want to know the child's religious affiliation. If this has not been documented before, the MOU provides a document in which the parties can rely on for that information.

If the CP Med is with respect to custody and access, having information about the child's doctor, dentist, school, and religious affiliation can be helpful during custody-specific discussions later in the mediation. Medical/ Dental, Religion, and Education are the primary topics covered under the term "Custody" so if there has already been a decision about those items, that discussion becomes less challenging and less emotionally charged.

Much like date of separation, having a rough idea of when the CAS file opened and reason for service may also provide insight as to how long the family has been struggling with the issue at hand. It also provides an opportunity to explore any changes that have occurred during that time and specifically, any progress the family has made.

SHUTTLE MEDIATION

Shuttle mediation is when the parties are in separate rooms, and the mediator travels back-and-forth. Reasons for using shuttle mediation include but are not limited to:

- one person's fear of another party
- possible physical intimidation
- physical and/ or emotional safety
- high level of conflict → it may be beneficial for the mediator to share the information in an effort to take the emotionality out of the content
- issues involving a support person → seeing them may create increased emotionality/ conflict

When using shuttle mediation, the mediator needs to review some guidelines with the parties at the beginning of the joint mediation session. Some guidelines include but are not limited to:

- no party will try to enter the room of any of the other parties unless approved by the mediator, and with the mediator present
- leaving the room (eg smoke breaks, bathroom breaks, etc) should be strategized with the mediator in an effort to avoid the parties from being in contact with each other. This is particularly important if the mediator thinks either of the parties may leave the building at any time.
- reminding parties that there may be extended periods of time when the mediator is not in the room, and with the

other party. Time with each party may not always be equal, and will vary based on the issues being discussed.

If the mediation involves parents on opposing sides, the worker generally travels back-and-forth with the mediator in a shuttle mediation. Often during a custody and access CP Med, the bulk of the negotiation is done between the parents. The worker is there to provide suggestions and also to intercept any plans that may be unsuitable in their estimation. As a result, the worker needs to be privy to the dialogue. The parties can however, still have conversations with the mediator without the worker present. When reviewing the ATM, remind parties that during a shuttle mediation, content disclosed in one room is shareable in the other room, unless the party asks that it not be shared.

If facilitating a shuttle mediation, the ATM to is reviewed in each room. The background information is also reviewed in each room. When one of the parties provides background information to the mediator, clarify its accuracy with the other party. If there are any discrepancies, the mediator needs to discuss this with the parties. If the parties cannot agree on the specifics of any background information, it should not be included in the MOU.

JOINT SESSION CONCLUSION

At the end of a successful mediation, the mediator will review the points of agreement with the parties. This ensures that there are no surprises when the parties receive the MOU. The mediator can provide any necessary clarification, and give the parties an idea of how the MOU will be written.

The end of the mediation session is another opportunity to remind the parties of their equality in the mediation process. Ask the parties how they would like to receive the MOU, and inform them that it will be sent to all of the parties via the same delivery method. That way, there is no perception of favouritism amongst the parties. If any of the parties requests that the MOU be sent via traditional mail, the MOU should be sent to all parties via traditional mail. This is because traditional mail is generally a slower mode of delivery than electronic methods (eg. email, fax).

Nowadays, the most common method of delivery is via email. When sending the MOU via email, ensure the parties are told at the joint mediation session that you will not make substantive changes to the MOU via email. The mediator may make corrections to details (ie wrong date, spelling error etc), but changes to the actual content of the agreement should not be amended outside of the actual mediation sessions. Changing the MOU based on an email from only one person can fuel conflict unnecessarily.

When planning to email parties, discuss whether or not their individual email addresses may be displayed in the address bar. When emailing multiple parties at the same time during the intake phase, it is best to ensure that addresses are blind copied. At the joint mediation session, privately ask for consent to display email addresses. If all of the parties consent to their address being displayed, the mediator may display the addresses. Then, the parties may "Reply To All" if there is a correction to be made on the MOU, and everyone is aware of the dialogue.

If there is going to be another joint mediation session, this is the ideal time to schedule the appointment. With technology today, most people have their cell phone with them, and their calendar is on their phone. Discussing upcoming appointments is easiest in real-time, and not via emails and phone calls after the fact.

Joint mediations sessions can be emotionally challenging and emotionally charged. Depending on the dynamics between the parties, it may be useful to have them leave at separate times. This is especially true in a shuttle mediation. In a shuttle mediation, the mediator should first wrap up with the at-risk person/ person who requested shuttle mediation. That will give them an opportunity to leave the area while the mediator is finishing up with the other person.

Not all mediations end on a positive note. There are times when one of the parties will end the process, and times when the mediator ends the process. Oftentimes when a client ends the process, they will leave the room and/ or building ahead of everyone. More often than not, the party is angry or frustrated. When this happens, it is important to debrief with the remaining parties to discuss safety when leaving. If there are concerns for safety, the other parties should be escorted to their vehicles, or have someone pick them up. In some instances it may be necessary to contact police to ask for assistance.

If the mediator ends the mediation, the mediator should debrief with each of the parties. The mediator should be careful as to what information they provide the parties, and be careful not to place blame on anyone. It is acceptable for the mediator to explain that mediation is ending because the mediator does not believe the parties will come to an agreement.

SUBSEQUENT JOINT MEDIATION SESSION(S)

It is rare that a CP Med is "completed" in one joint mediation session. In fact, it often takes several meetings. There are some mediators who break their mediations into several one hour appointments. Personally, I book three hours for the first appointment, and each subsequent appointment is usually two hours long. Of course, this is flexible depending on the dynamics of the case, and the clients involved. Not everyone can manage long appointments; especially with such emotionally charged topics. I prefer longer appointments, as it gives time to get into a rhythm with the family, and have in-depth conversation. Also, there is little chance of feeling rushed.

All of the scheduling and safety dynamics discussed earlier still apply for subsequent meetings. As parties arrive for subsequent joint mediation sessions, best practice is to meet with each client privately for a few moments to do a check-in. Review any significant events since the last session, discuss the implementation of the agreement since the last session, and get a sense of what the parties want to discuss on that day. This may also create an opportunity for the mediator to give the clients suggestions on how to handle possible challenges that may be forthcoming.

When the meeting begins, ask the clients if there are any corrections from the previous MOU. This includes spelling errors, clarification on wording, etc. Once this has been addressed, ask for an update from the clients on what has happened since the last appointment. You will have a sense of this from the check-ins, but what they say in the group setting will also give some insight into the power dynamics between the parties. It is important to know if the parties have been successful in implementing previous strategies, and if there are adjustments that need to be made. This will begin discussion on items that need to be revisited, and any new business.

Often while writing the MOU after the first session, I think of topics that I believe the family should discuss. When this happens, I make a note in the file. During a subsequent joint session, I mention the topic. Some mediators keep a list of topics with them in every file. I think this is a great idea; especially in a Family Mediation. It is important however, to remember that CP Med cases are generally more dynamic than a traditional Family Mediation. As a result, the cookie-cutter approach is unlikely to work.

MEMORANDUM OF UNDERSTANDING

The Memorandum of Understanding (MOU) is the document that the mediator sends to the parties following the mediation. It is a list of agreements reached in principle. In a CP Med, it does not list any of the items of which the parties did not agree. The MOU is not legally binding when the mediator sends it, and the mediator should NOT be having clients sign the MOU in their presence.

At the end of the joint mediation session(s), parties are once again directed to get legal advice. They should have a lawyer review the MOU, and give their opinion on its contents. A lawyer will ensure that the participant fully understands the document, and its implications. The lawyer will also offer suggestions on any items that need further discussion or changes.

The MOU is a flexible document. Parties have the ability to change their mind on any of its contents. The mediator should however, encourage the parties to inform one another if they intend on making changes. If the parties make changes to how they will act out the MOU without informing the other parties, it will lead to further conflict.

Although the MOU is not legally binding, it does become an expectation of CAS. If parties make changes in the implementation of the MOU without informing CAS, they should be prepared for CAS to follow up and ask questions.

Different mediators have different approaches to the structure of the MOU. Some believe that it should be written in plain language. They believe that terms with legal connotations such as "shall" should be replaced with "will." Although these words have the same meaning, some mediators feel using the word "shall" makes the MOU sound too much like a legal document.

There are other mediators however, who prefer to use legal terminology and language. Their feeling is that it will be more cost effective for the clients after the fact to have the MOU made into a legally-binding document. Regardless of your approach, the most important thing to remember is that the MOU needs to be written in a way that clients, including family members, understand.

When sending the MOU via email, it is best to send the file in pdf format. Some mediators will also encrypt the document as an added safety measure. Sending the MOU in pdf format makes it more difficult for the parties to edit the document. Ultimately, the MOU is the clients' document, and it is "in principle." So, any of the clients may change any of the points of the MOU to whatever suits them best. For the mediator however, they should make attempts to protect the content, so anything with their name on it is actually their words.

The MOU should only be sent to a party's lawyer with the consent of the party.

FIRST NATIONS, INUIT, MÉTIS

As mentioned, children who are First Nations, Inuk, or Métis are entitled to services specific to their communities. Unfortunately, the CYFSA does not specifically define the terms First Nations, Inuk/ Inuit, or Métis, and they are not terms included in the Indian Act. It can be surmised that it would include a child who belongs to a First Nations, Inuit, or Métis community, or a child who identifies with a First Nations, Inuit, or Métis community. As a result, it is not necessary for the child to have "Status." Of note, the term *Status* is not used in the CYFSA or the Indian Act with respect to individuals of First Nations, Inuit, or Métis heritage. As of 2018, the Indian Act identifies First Nations people with Status as "Registered Indians." I suspect this will change.

When considering ADR for a child of First Nations, Inuit, or Métis heritage, CAS must consult with a representative of the child's Band. This consultation is to enquire if the Band has established their own ADR process. If so, they worker is required to inform the family of the Indigenous Alternative Dispute Resolution (IADR) process. Best practice would be to have the representative from the Band assist in the explanation of the IADR process. Once the family is informed of the different processes, it is then the family's choice as to whether or not they wish to participate in an IADR, CP Med or a hybrid.

Once the family has made their choice, it is the responsibility of the CAS to inform the representative of the Band of the family's choice. If the family has chosen CP Med, CAS must also inform the representative once the referral has been submitted. Section 73 of the CYFSA mandates the CAS to "consult with a representative" and as a result, CAS does not require the family to sign a consent form to share this information.

When discussing First Nations, Inuit, or Métis heritage, the CYFSA refers to the child, and not the parent. Discussions about the child's heritage should be focussed on the child, and with whom they identify. Although one of the parents may be of First Nations, Inuit, or Métis heritage, the child may not identify with those communities. As a result, there is not an obligation to explore First Nations, Inuit, or Métis services in those circumstances.

NARRATIVE:

A worker consulted with me with respect to a file in which the father had First Nations heritage, and was a member of a local Band. The mother was not of First Nations heritage, and the children also did not have "Status." The family was requesting mediation, but also wanted an Indigenous component. As a result, the file was referred for CP Med, and I facilitated the process alongside an IADR facilitator, *Linda*.

Although I had coordinated hybrid models with IADR and FGDM, I had never done a CP Med - IADR hybrid before. *Linda* and I consulted with each other as soon as the referral arrived. She was not trained as a CP Mediator, so I explained some of the necessary steps in the CP Med process; specifically those with respect to screening and safety. *Linda* also shared with me some of the necessary steps in an IADR to ensure that I honoured any of the family's traditions.

The first party I contacted as part of the process was Dad. I wanted to clarify that the referral had been sent for CP Med, but also to confirm that he was seeking an IADR component. He confirmed that the family was looking for mediation, but that they were also wanting First Nations support. With that information, I was able to begin the process, and scheduled his intake appointment.

Prior to Dad's intake appointment, *Linda* and I met to strategize our approach for that day. To our surprise, Dad arrived for his intake appointment with Mum and their three year old child. Prior to that, I had not been able to reach the mother to schedule her intake appointment. There was insufficient time to conduct a thorough intake appointment with each of them, so *Linda* and I did not proceed with intakes at that time. Instead, we used the time to inform both parties about the process, and to answer any process-related questions. At the end, we privately booked their individual intake appointments.

During our information session with the parents, it was clear that both of them were open to receiving services from the Band of which Dad belonged. As a result, *Linda* reached out to the Band, and informed them that we had begun our process. The Band was very open to working with us, and respectful that we would reach out after all of the intake appointments were completed. At that time, we would have a better understanding of the family's needs.

After completing of the intakes and determining that the mediation would move forward, *Linda* and I planned a follow-up with the Band Representative (Rep). Through our discussion however, we realized that we did not get consent from the parents during their intake appointments to disclose information about their situation to the Band Rep. Sharing this information was necessary for the Band to determine what services they had available, and were willing to provide. As a result, *Linda* and I had to add a step to our process by getting a signed consent from each parent. What we should have done is had the consent signed at the initial intake appointment with each parent.

Once we had signed consent from both parents, *Linda* followed up with the Band Rep, and we booked a conference call with them. During our call however, the Band Rep was upset that they had not heard about the CP Med referral until *Linda* had contacted them. I felt like things were going to unravel quickly, and reminded the Band Rep that the issue was with CAS; not *Linda* and myself. Thankfully, this misstep in process did not derail things.

The Band Rep attended for the joint mediation session, and we started the session with a smudging ceremony led by the Band Rep. In many First Nations communities, smudging is a ritual cleansing performed at the beginning of meetings. The purpose is to remind people to enter into the process with good intent. As the smoke rises and is passed over the body, negative energy, negative feelings, and negative emotions are lifted away. After smudging, much of the joint mediation session ran like any other.

This example demonstrates the need for mediators to be flexible in their thinking. This family had very specific wants and needs and because of flexible thinking, *Linda* and I were able to help them. By bringing in the Band Rep, we were also able to access family supports that may not have otherwise been available. All of this combined empowered the family to make decisions that met the needs of their children.

OPENNESS
MEDIATION

Openness Mediation (OM) is another specialized form of mediation. Once trained as a CP Mediator, there is additional training through OAFM that is specific to OM. In order to receive the designation of Specialist in OM, the CP Mediator is required to take a two-day comprehensive training. The training reviews legislation specific to adoption and openness, and also reviews the OM process. OM training is not mandatory to conduct Openness Mediations, but it is highly recommended.

Openness is not a new idea. It has existed for many years in many cultures, and has also long been the norm in private adoptions. In child welfare, there has historically been a presumption that when a child was adopted, that child would no longer have contact with their birth family. Nowadays, that has become more challenging.

As children get older, they naturally begin to ask questions about their heritage. When they learn that they were adopted, they often begin to ask questions about their birth family. It is becoming easier for birth families to connect as a result of social media. Although there are wonderful success stories, there are also horror stories in which people have taken advantage of one-another's vulnerabilities. The concept of OM is to ensure that the child has some connection with their birth family, but in a safe and meaningful way.

Some of the benefits of openness include, but are not limited to:
- children experience less sense of loss through the adoptive process
- decrease in adolescent identity issues
- creates a link for adoptive parents and children to learn about potential familial health issues if necessary
- helps birth families process grief and loss as they are part of the decision-making process with respect to the child's placement

Openness does not mean access. It means contact. True, contact may be physical contact (ie access) with the birth family. But it may also be much more limited (eg pictures once per year). There is no limit to the amount of contact, but there is also no presumption as to a minimum standard. Ultimately, the level of contact must be in the child's best interests, and within the realm of functional possibilities for the adoptive family. If the birth family lives in Thunder Bay, Ontario and the adoptive family lives in Toronto, weekly physical contact is not a functional possibility; especially if nobody has the ability to drive.

LEGISLATION

Adoption creates another level of separation from the birth family. In Extended Society Care, it is the CAS who is the child's legal guardian. With adoption, those legal rights are legally transferred to another person through the courts, and that person legally becomes the child's parent. Part VIII of the CYFSA specifically deals with adoption, and openness is noted in multiple sections of the Act.

Although Extended Society Care is a loss of parental rights, many parents continue to have access with children during this time. Once adopted however, all previous access orders are terminated. Although openness is encouraged, there is no presumption that physical contact will continue between the child and the birth family post-adoption.

Luckily, there is now mechanism to discuss contact with the family, and encourage it. As mention, in the past, the child welfare adoption process had a starting point where there was to be no contact with the birth family. Now however, the starting point is that openness must be considered in all adoptions. Section 185(2) of the CYFSA states:

Where a society begins planning for the adoption of a child who is in extended society care under an order made under paragraph 3 of subsection 101 (1) or clause 116 (1) (c), the society shall consider the benefits of an openness order or openness agreement in respect of the child.

The CYFSA continues that the purpose of Openness Orders and Openness Agreements is "facilitating communication or maintaining a relationship between the child and..." important people in their life. Important people may include:
- members of the birth family (eg. parent, sibling)
- a person with whom the child has a significant relationship or emotional tie (eg. foster parent, extended family)
- or a member of the child's community who will help the child develop of maintain a connection with their heritage and cultural identity

REFERRAL

As in more traditional forms of CP Med, the OM referral is generally initiated by the CAS. The referral may be made before placement in the adoptive home, after placement in the adoptive home and sometimes, even after the adoption has been finalized. Along with the referral for OM, CAS must also send a referral to the OCL. In most cases when a child has become a child in Extended Society Care, there has been previous OCL involvement. As a result, the lawyer previously assigned is likely to be the child's lawyer during OM.

INTAKE

Worker

As noted, the order in which intake appointments occur in more traditional CP Meds should be random. In OM however, intake appointments should begin with the worker. This is so the mediator may gain a better understanding of the case history, adoption disclosure, availability of post-adoption services, and the parties' understanding of openness.

Proposed goals of the mediation are less important to gather because based on a referral for OM, there is an understanding that openness is the goal. Each party's perceived understanding of openness however is very important information to gather. It is very common for birth families to have a view that openness means access. For adoptive families however, openness may not mean any physical contact.

Based on the expertise of the CAS and their experience with the parties, they have already made a determination that the file is appropriate for Openness. So, the mediator is not screening for suitability for Openness. The mediator is however screening for suitability for mediation. When meeting with the worker, the mediator should enquire about:
- competence of the parties (ie significant mental health)
- no contact/ restraining orders, etc
- threats of violence or retaliation
- Openness Order or Openness Agreement
- services available to the adoptive and birth families after the mediation and adoption finalization

An adoption worker in Toronto, Jay Lomax, has created an adoption ceremony for children who belong to or identify with a

First Nations, Inuit, or Métis community. Although this is only formally in place for indigenous children at this time, it is worth asking the worker if there are any ceremonies planned to commemorate the adoption. If so, there should also be discussion as to whether or not the birth family would be invited to participate.

Power Imbalances

One of the items the mediator is also not assessing is power imbalances. By virtue of a child being adopted, there is a significant power imbalance shifted towards the adoptive family. Ultimately, they have the ability to say yes or no to whatever suits their wants and needs. This is a difficult obstacle to overcome, but understanding the positions of the parties will help the mediator better prepare for the joint sessions.

Openness Orders are court orders with respect to ongoing contact between the child and someone with whom they have a meaningful relationship. There are two sets of circumstances in which an application for an openness order may be made:

1. There is no order for access to a child in Extended Society Care who will be placed for adoption. In this situation, the CAS would apply for an openness order.
2. There is an order for access to a child in Extended Society Care who is to be placed for adoption. In this situation, the person previously granted access would apply for an openness order.

Openness Agreements can happen at any time (before or after adoption), and are arranged outside of court. They are agreements negotiated by the adoptive family and typically the birth family.

They may however include other individuals with whom the child has a meaningful relationship.

Essentially, the MOU that the mediator prepares following OM is an Openness Agreement. It is then the decision of the parties as to whether or not they file the MOU with the court, and have it made into an Openness Order. Because the agreement is not an order, there is more flexibility to make changes outside of court in the event of a change in circumstances (eg relocation, child's wishes, etc). Conversely, openness agreements are not enforceable by the courts in the event of a break-down.

First Nations, Inuit, or Métis

Much like a typical CP Med, the mediator needs to ask questions of the worker as to whether or not the child belongs to or identifies with a First Nations, Inuit, or Métis community. If the answer is yes, Section 186 of the CYFSA states:

The society shall give written notice of its intention to a representative chosen by each of the child's Bands and First Nations, Inuit or Métis communities.

The intention is with respect to the child being adopted. This notice is to give the First Nations, Inuit, or Métis community an opportunity to explore placement options within their community.

Adoptive Family and Birth Family

The order in which adoptive or birth family members are met is not as important. In addition to the typical CP Med intake screening process, the mediator should also review issues like mobility, what the client needs to know about the birth/ adoptive family, and the

141

difference between an Agreement and an Order. Ideally, the parties will have Independent Legal Advice to review Agreement vs. Order, but best practice is to review the differences with the clients. This is also helpful for the mediator as the more information you review with the clients, the better equipped you are to manage those question during the joint mediation sessions.

The mediator should also review what Openness truly means. Many will confuse the term openness with access. This may give birth families false hope, and may also create increased stress and anxiety for the adoptive family. When meeting with each, be clear to review the parameters of Openness and that although it may be physical contact, it may also be limited to one-directional picture sharing at pre-determined intervals.

Because of the complexities of OM and the emotionality, it is possible that birth family members may require an additional intake session prior to the joint mediation session. This may be necessary to allow them to process that openness does not mean access, and that in spite of openness, an adoption order is a final order.

Adoptive Family

Oftentimes, OM occurs after the child has gone to live with the adoptive family. This is generally referred to as adoption probation. When meeting with the adoptive family for their intake, ask them to prepare "A Day In The Life of..." for the joint mediation session. This may include the child's daily routines in their home, demonstrated interests, milestones (eg started walking, lost teeth, learned to skate, learned to print their name etc), struggles, and anything else the adoptive family thinks will give the birth family a picture of how the child is doing in the adoptive home.

If the adoptive family and birth family have never met before, ask the adoptive family to consider preparing a profile about themselves. The hope is that the birth family can keep this profile, and that it will help them find some peace that their child is being placed in a healthy, happy, and safe environment. Information about the adoptive family's address or contact information should only be shared if the adoptive family is comfortable with sharing that information.

If the adoptive parents have plans to give anything to the birth parents, remind the adoptive parents to make a copy for the child as well. In the future, it will demonstrate what efforts the adoptive family made to support everyone in the adoption process.

Birth Family

When meeting with the birth family, ask them to prepare an update about their life situation. This may include things like recent health diagnoses, career changes, significant family events and treatment for addictions or mental health concerns. Also, ask them to share information about any important family traditions, and their hopes and dreams for the child. Birth family members should also be reminded that the joint mediation session is not a forum to protest the adoption. That decision has been made, and is not open for further discussion. The purpose of the mediation is to explore openness.

Children's Lawyer

In the OM training manual, the recommendation is that you meet with the OCL last. This is to allow the OCL sufficient time to meet with their client. This of course, is dependent on how long it has been since the child entered into Extended Society Care. Almost without exception, an OCL would have been appointed for a child prior to entering Extended Society Care. If the OCL has remained actively involved with the child since the Extended Society Care order, it is not necessary to meet with them last. If the OCL has been newly appointed or it has been a significant time since the Extended Society Care order, it is best to meet the OCL last.

In addition to obtaining the child's views and preferences, it is also important to ask the OCL if the child is consenting to the adoption. Section 180(6) of the CYFSA states *An order for the adoption of a person who is seven or older shall not be made without the person's written consent.* Although a formality, it should be noted in the mediator's file.

JOINT SESSION

Ideally, the joint mediation session should be held outside of a CAS location. Oftentimes, birth families hold resentment towards CAS for removing the child, and there may also be trauma related to the removal. Holding the joint mediation session at CAS may trigger some of those feelings. This in turn, may create further barriers to agreement and relationship building between the birth family and adoptive family.

Although CAS must be present for the joint mediation session, the bulk of the negotiations are between the adoptive family and the birth family. The role of CAS in the joint mediation session is that of a support. They may provide suggestions on how best to move forward, and how they will provide support after the adoption is finalized.

At the beginning of the joint mediation session, it is useful to point out that people are likely nervous about the process. For some, it may be the first time the birth family and adoptive family have ever met. By identifying the nervousness that both sides are no doubt feeling, it acts as a reminder that compassion is necessary through the meeting. There should also be mention that the objective of the day is to remain focussed on the well-being of the child, and that the mediator will remind people of this throughout the meeting.

Once the Agreement To Mediate has been reviewed and signed, the OCL should be asked to present the views and preferences of the child. Next, the adoptive family and birth family may share their individual updates and "A Day In The Life Of..." The order in which things occur during the joint mediation session is strategic. By reviewing the child's views and preferences first, it reminds parties that the child is the focus. Also, the information sharing among the parties prevents the parties from jumping right into negotiations. The intent of the meeting is to hopefully build relationships, and generate conversation. The information sharing creates a platform for those discussions.

If the parties intend on exchanging any gifts or pictures, this is best done at the end of the joint mediation session. Ending the meeting can be very challenging, because it may also symbolize a more significant end for the birth family. The exchange of gifts, or pictures can help strengthen the bond between the adoptive family and birth family. Although they may not have regular contact with each other, they still remain connected through the child. So, a positive experience is incredibly useful.

TOOL BOX

CULTURE FLOWER EXERCISE

Executive Director of Peel Family Mediation Services and Presenter on Cultural Diversity, Antoinette Clarke suggests that one way to learn more about a person's culture is with the use of a "Culture Flower" or "Cultural Matrix." She suggests giving the clients an opportunity to write down their thoughts and ideas about who they are, and how this might affect the power dynamics within the mediation process. Examples of an individual's cultural identity include, but are not limited to:

- Canadian/ American/ British...
- Heterosexual/ Homosexual/ Transgender...
- mother/ father/ brother/ sister/ parent/ child...
- Christian/ Jewish/ Agnostic...
- mediator/ ironworker/ stay-at-home parent...

In my practice, I provide people with a clipboard and the image in *Figure 3* while they are in the waiting room immediately before their intake appointment. Although I provide people with various intake and screening questionnaires in advance of their appointment, I leave the culture flower until immediately before the appointment. This is because I want their answers to be spontaneous, and not well thought out. I believe this mimics some of the conversation dynamics in a joint mediation session. Although it is generally much less emotionally charged before an intake appointment, beginning the exercise then provides a more honest picture of the cultural paradigm from which the person operates.

Once the client completes the flower, we begin the intake appointment, and go through much of the screening process detailed earlier. I leave the exercise until the end of the conversation in hopes that rapport has been built. As a heterosexual white male, it can sometimes be challenging to have conversations about culture with individuals in a safe way.

Figure 3: Culture Flower

Image developed by Dr Michael Heintz, and used with permission

The text above the image simply says "Please fill in the spaces with characteristics that you consider important in explaining the type of person you are." Initially, I was expecting answers similar to those outlined earlier. I was surprised when I start getting answers such as:
- helpful
- caring
- honest
- straight-forward
- trustworthy
- fair

Initially, I struggled to accept these answers because to me, they did not reflect the desired outcome of the exercise; to explore an individual's culture. This emphasized a bias in me that it is not my role to define a client's culture. It is their job to do so. I realized that the term Culture is a Global term. It relates to an individual's sense of belonging to a previously defined social group. Although this is important, the answers above were Local. They provided insight into how the individual viewed their self concept. Although not what was intended, it still provides valuable information.

In Ms Clarke's exercise, she provides clients with examples. I do not. Ms Clarke's exercise points clients in the direction of the answers to which she is seeking. This has significant benefit as it initiates a conversation about culture. By not providing examples however, the client will provide examples of what the term "characteristics" means to them. It may also highlight some cultural differences as some cultures may be more inclined to include their Social Identity whereas others may list their Self Concept. It will be up to you to determine which method best meets your needs and the needs of your clients in the mediation process.

Client Review

When reviewing the Culture Flower with the client, show them the image again to refresh their memory. Then, ask open-ended questions about what the answers mean, and why they put the answers in their specific location. Some answers about location may simply be "because it fit there," whereas others may have very specific reasons.

Why This Image?

Although you could use any variety of images to reflect this concept, I use the image in *Figure 3* for very specific reasons. The flower has nine petals from which to choose. That provides the clients with lots of options as how they wish to define themselves. There is a centre circle which people will often use to place their most valuable identity and within each petal, there is a small circle. Sometimes, clients may divide their identity.

For example, they may place 'Man' in one petal but in one of the smaller circles, they may place 'Father.' To them, father is a sub-set of man. For others, they may put 'Man' and 'Father' in different petals all together. When reviewing the image with clients, explore what the items mean to them; not you as a practitioner.

Mediation Affect

Once you have an understanding of what the answers mean to the client, follow up with questions about each item, and how they will impact the joint mediation session. The original intent of the exercise was to explore power differentials in the mediation process. By expanding the "correct" responses to include self concept, the mediator becomes better prepared to navigate the dynamics of the joint mediation session, as it provides even more information about each individual client.

COMMUNICATION-CONFLICT WAVE

It is not uncommon for clients to comment that the mediator is asking them to add a lot of extra detail to their MOU. There is a reason for this. Although some clients may be communicating well with each other at that time, there have likely been times in the past that the parties have not communicated well. After all, they're in mediation for a reason. Given this information, it is also very likely that there will be periods of time in the future in which the clients will not communicate well. Oftentimes when clients are not communicating well, they are engaged in higher conflict. That's where the Communication-Conflict Wave comes in.

An MOU needs to be a functional document, and the Communication-Conflict Wave helps clients visualize this concept. The MOU needs to be detailed, yet leave room for the parties to be flexible in the document's implementation if they choose to be flexible. If the document is too rigid, it is not functional. The opposite is also true. If the document is too vague, it is also not functional.

An example of document rigidity would be a schedule that sets out very specific and strict exchange times. Although most family law professionals would say this is a good thing, the dilemma is that sometimes life happens. Without flexible language to allow for the parties to make changes, the parties become prisoners of the MOU. This in turn creates further resentment and conflict amongst the clients.

An example of wording that is too vague would be "reasonable access with reasonable notice." The definition of reasonable to one person may not be the same as to the other person. This lack of detail further sets the parties up for conflict. Fortunately in recent years, we have become much better in our facilitation of family matters and this *reasonable* clause is rarely seen nowadays.

As can be seen in *Figure 4*, one line represents Communication and the other represents Conflict. The lines work in opposition with one another. Generally speaking, when conflict is high among parties, effective communication is low. Conversely, when effective communication is high, conflict is generally low.

Figure 4: Communication-Conflict Wave

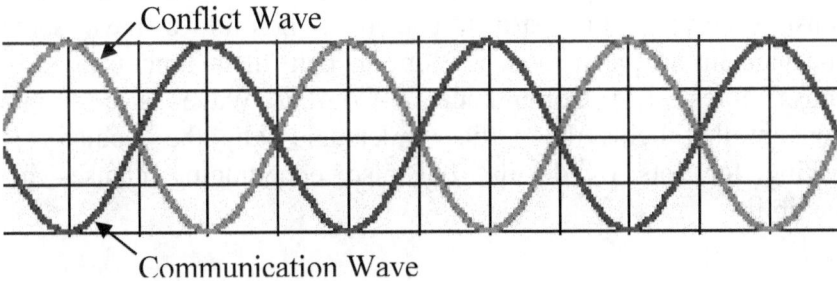

The concept of the Communication-Conflict Wave helps clients visualize a functional MOU. If they are experiencing periods of high conflict, the terms of their agreement are set. The expectations are clearly outlined, and they do not require communication. Conversely, when parties are communicating more positively, there is flexibility built into the MOU to allow for them to make changes if they all agree.

An example of flexible wording would include detailed pick-up and drop-off times and locations, but also a paragraph such as *"The parties may make changes to the schedule provided they both agree in advance of the proposed change."* In this example, the parties may make changes to the detailed schedule, however they must agree before the change takes effect. If they do not agree, the implication is that the original schedule remains in place. It also outlines that both parties are required to consent to the change, and one party cannot arbitrarily make the change on their own.

LIFE IS A PROCESS; NOT AN EVENT

Relationships are non-linear. They do not travel in a straight line, and are often described as "up and down." Although the parties may be getting along and are amicable during the mediation, life happens. There may be circumstances in the future that creates tension between the parties, and it is helpful to have some mechanisms in place ahead of time to help them function during those times. The Communication-Conflict Wave is a simple concept that helps the parties understand why the mediator is asking for lots of details, but also encouraging clauses for flexibility.

FAMILY TRIANGLE EXERCISE

The Family Triangle is an effective tool in helping families shift their focus from the past to the present, and ultimately, to the future. While family relationships are complex, the Family Triangle provides a simplistic visual representation of the child-parent-parent relationship. It is useful in helping parents understand how they are forever connected through their child, and how their interactions have an impact on the child.

The concept of the Family Triangle is just that; a simple triangle. One point represents the child, while the other two points each represent a parent. Further, the points are connected. The Family Triangle can further be utilized to visualize and discuss other triadic relationships including but not limited to:

- child-grandparent-parent
- child-child-caregiver
- employee-supervisor-employer

Client Exercise: Genealogy

The Family Triangle is a visual exercise. When explaining the Family Triangle to parents, ask them questions about their lineage. Ask them to describe a genogram, and where they want to place people on the page or board. In most cases, they will suggest that the child is at the bottom, and the ancestors are higher up on the page. Once you have gone through a few generations, ask the parents if they see anything of concern with the diagram and specifically, if they have concerns with where people are located. As a mediator, it is important to be patient and comfortable with silence to allow individuals time to consider the questions, and to contemplate their responses.

After some time, specifically call their attention to where the child is in the diagram. In most cases, the child will be placed on the bottom of the genogram. In Western cultures, we read from the top of the page, and usually write our most important ideas first. By putting the child at the bottom, it visually implies that they are less important. In our line of work, our primary focus is on the well-being of the child so as a result, they should be on the top of our diagram. They are the most important "item" for discussion throughout the mediation process. Also remind clients that by the child being on the bottom of *their* diagram, the child is also bearing the weight and biases of all of those ancestors before them and above them.

The concept of carrying the weight of our ancestors is somewhat abstract, and difficult for some to conceptualize. With each generation, there are biases and prejudices that affect our interactions with others. Most importantly, those biases and prejudices affect how people parent as individuals and within a parent-group. The impact of those biases and prejudices are then passed down to the next generation. The affected generation may or may not pass the information down further, but it does shape their thought processes and decision-making.

That in turn creates an emotional weight that impacts their abilities to interact with others. It becomes further complicated when friends and extended family members (ie "Cheerleaders") add input directly to the situation. If the child is exposed to this input, it has the potential to create even more emotional weight on the child. With them figuratively on the bottom, this emotional weight can become crushing over time. (The concept of "Cheerleaders" will be covered in more detailed).

With the child at the bottom, it also presents as the parents being the most important people in the family system. This creates an environment wherein progress is stalled, or breaks down completely. Parents become fixated on being right or winning, instead of focussed on the well-being of the child. The mediation becomes parent-centred and will fail. Using the Family Triangle helps clients further understand that the focus of the conversation needs to be on the child.

With the Family Triangle, the child is at the top. Ask the clients why they are in mediation, and what they are looking to discuss. When they respond with "the child," ask them again where that child should be on the paper. Affirm that the child should be at the top of the page. When reviewing this concept on paper, it is helpful to literally spin the page so the child is at the top.

Figure 5: Family Triangle

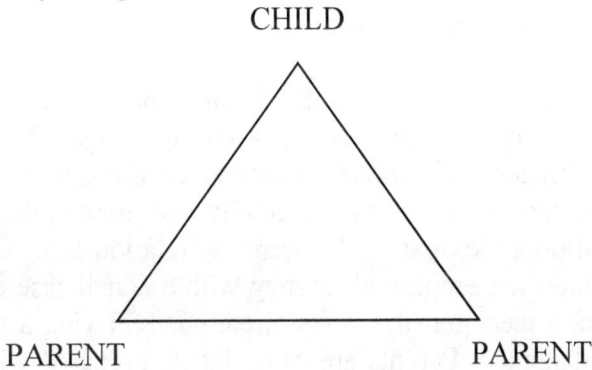

Visualizing the triangle in this way allows people to view the relationship from a structural perspective. There is a base (a foundation), a distinct top (a purpose), and everyone is connected. This makes it easier for people to understand the concept, and helps facilitate change in their parenting relationship. Unlike the typical family hierarchy, this image more closely parallels the dynamics in a family group. There is a strong base at the bottom, with an apex reaching for the sky. If children are told "The Sky Is The Limit," parents have an obligation to help the child reach for that goal. This is accomplished by working cooperatively, and providing the child with the necessary foundation.

Post-Exercise Discussion: Communication

The Family Triangle illustrates basic connections that must exist in a child-parent-parent group. While all of the lines are important, in mediation, special focus is often needed on the connection between the parents. From a functional perspective, it represents communication, understanding of differences, and support of each other. It is also acknowledging that even though the romantic relationship has ended, the parental relationship must continue. It emphasizes genuinely putting the needs of the child above the wants and needs of the parents.

As shown in *Figure 5*, The Family Triangle has the child at the top with the parents as the base. As children age, they become physically bigger and heavier. Often over time, their emotional weight also increases. This is especially true for families engaged in a tumultuous "ex-partner" parenting relationship. Think of a child starting their emotional journey with a pencil case and by the time they're a teenager, they may already be carrying a suitcase of emotional baggage. Parents are often left unprepared with how to deal with the backlash of that baggage and unfortunately, they are often significant contributors to the weight of that baggage.

As the base of The Family Triangle, the parents remain as the support for the child; constantly trying to prop them up and help them reach their goals. The dilemma is that without functional and productive communication between the parents, there is nothing keeping the child's base points connected and secure. Over time, with lack of communication and lack of understanding, the base points slide further and further apart. Eventually, the base can no longer support the peak, and the child emotionally crashes to the ground.

It is also important to note that regardless of the parenting relationship, there is a necessity to get information from one parent to the other. If there is not effective communication among the adults (ie no base connection), there is only one route for that information to get to the other parent. That is through the child. This again increases that emotional weight, and entrenches the child in the conflict among the parents. Long-term effects of this include, but are not limited to:

- increased stress on child
- parentification of child
- resentment in the child towards the parents
- child terminates relationship with parents once old enough

Another common issue with this break-down in communication relates to the manipulation of information. When parents don't speak, children may change the content of the information being relayed. This may be a direct result of intentional manipulation, or it may be a simple misunderstanding. In reality, some parents are asking children to share information of which they do not have the intellect to comprehend. As a result, the information becomes distorted. This further complicates matters when there is a response required by the other parent. Their response is based on misinformation and furthermore, their response may be adjusted by the child as well. It becomes an issue of broken telephone. The outcome again, increases the emotional weight of the child.

Figure 6:

It is through this simple illustration (*Figure 6*) that many parents come to a realization about their family group. To keep the base points from sliding further apart and the child from emotionally crashing to the ground, parents need to maintain functional and productive communication with each other. They do not need to be in constant communication, but they need to demonstrate an ability to communicate effectively to show the child they are working together in the child's best interests.

In my office, I have heard a plethora reasons why parents "cannot" communicate with each other. They feel the other person doesn't listen. Sometimes they feel the other person doesn't take them seriously or even care about their opinion. I have even heard parents actually say that they hate each other. Using the Family Triangle is not an exercise to promote direct communication. It is an exercise to promote effective communication. Sometimes, this is accomplished by external means such as mediation, parenting coordination, and communication software (eg My Family Wizard).

I would venture a guess that although communication through lawyers often relays important information, it rarely promotes effective communication amongst the parents. Communication through lawyers often includes complex legal terms that a lay person may not understand. Furthermore, communication through lawyers creates an adversarial sentiment, and further breaks down the communication base of the Family Triangle.

Post-Exercise Discussion: Parenting Styles

The Family Triangle can also be used to discuss healthy parenting styles, and the need for balance. Many clients express how the other parent has a different parenting style from them, and this causes great stress. The Family Triangle provides clinicians with a tool to help clients visualize the need for similarities and differences in their parenting. Similarities and differences in parenting styles are necessary whether parents are living in the same home or different homes.

Parents need to have some similarities in their parenting style, but they do not need to be identical. In fact, even in-tact families have parents with some differences in parenting styles. Variation is good! The slight variations in dealing with day-to-day issues help the child to adjust to variations they will encounter in the outside world. Using The Family Triangle demonstrates that if the styles are too similar, the base is too narrow. The structure is unstable and even though the child's emotional weight may not be as heavy, it takes very little to emotionally knock the child over (*Figure 7*).

Figure 7:

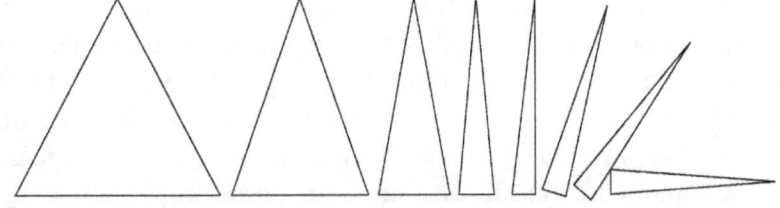

Conversely, if the parenting styles are significantly different, the base points of the triangle once again become too far apart. Although this visually appears to be a strong base, there is a point of diminishing returns. The extreme differences in the homes create a world of chaos for the child. They struggle to adapt because of the lack of consistency in their environments. This again increases the emotional weight of the child, and it becomes overwhelming for the base to support. As in *Figure 6*, the base slips out and once again, the child emotionally crumbles to the ground.

When discussing the Family Triangle with parents with respect to parenting styles, the conversation often shifts back to effective communication. It emphasizes that even when parents lived together, they had differences. When they had those differences, they spoke about them. Just because they are now living separately, it does not mean that effective communication has to end. In fact, effective communication may be even more necessary as parents are not both actively engaged in daily parenting. When referencing parenting styles, parents should have discussions about some of the differences and similarities in their homes. By doing so, they are demonstrating effective communication for their children, and further providing emotional stability by trying to parent cooperatively.

Conclusion

Clinicians are often looking for new, intricate ways of interacting with clients. Far too often however, the processes and strategies become complicated and confusing. Sometimes, the best teaching tools are the simplest teaching tools. Clients engaged in the mediation process are often emotionally drained by the time they enter into the process. By using a simple triangle, the message gets through without creating further stress or confusion.

CHEERLEADERS

A cheerleader is generally thought of as someone that cheers, chants, and dances in support of a sports team. Their job is to motivate and inspire the team so they continue to try their best right up until the end of the game, regardless of the score or consequences. Although they are focused on the same outcome (ie winning), their role is not to coach the team or actually play the sport. It is to encourage.

Cheerleaders exist in our personal lives as well. In family settings, they are the spouses, partners, siblings, extended family, and friends of the individuals involved in the mediation. Although it often feels good to have someone cheering us on, it can also have negative consequences when the cheerleader starts to shift their role to coaching. This is especially evident when the cheering contains bad advice, and is based on a lack of knowledge of the law or the individual dynamics of the situation.

The purpose of the cheerleader is to motivate the team to win. This should immediately raise flags. In family law, the motivation should not be to win. It should be to find peace, and to be the best parent of which you are capable. The idea of winning and losing further polarizes people in family law. It is helpful for mediators to remind participants that the goal is not to win, but to work cooperatively.

In the sporting analysis, cheerleaders continue their role regardless of the outcome of the game. They cheer on their team. They tell the team that they can win no matter how poorly the team is playing, and regardless of the decisions (good or bad) that are being made by the players or the coaches. I refer to family and friends as cheerleaders because regardless of how bad things are, they continue to encourage the client to fight to the bitter end.

Unfortunately, continued conflict in the family setting creates greater emotional discord, and often affects children negatively.

Although our cheerleaders mean well by encouraging us to continue the fight, they cannot fully understand the dynamics of the client's individual situation. Statements of empathy abound, but are rarely helpful; much like when a loved one dies. Examples of cheerleader statements include:
- I know how you feel
- I've been there
- this is what my ex and I did
- when I got separated, my lawyer told me...

When meeting with clients, I remind them that although their cheerleaders mean well, they are not the same person as my client. The cheerleaders did not have their yesterday. They were not involved with the same former partner. They do not have their children. They are not the ones sitting in that chair in my office; only my client is. As a result, the cheerleader cannot fully understand the feelings the client is experiencing, and they are ill-equipped to offer advice on how to manage the situation, especially if the cheerleader is neither a lawyer nor a therapist.

Using the sports analogy, mediators should remind clients to listen to their coach. Their lawyer is their coach and although it isn't their role to understand the client on an emotional level, they have an expertise in family law. As such, they are able to provide clients with the best advice and hopefully, direct them towards a healthier resolution.

CHEERLEADERS ARE NOT COACHES

In some therapeutic settings, clients are encouraged to be a cheerleader for themselves. My challenge to this is that cheerleaders stand on the sidelines. Clients need to be in the game.

To be the best player they can be, they need to listen to their coach for advice, accept the encouragement of their cheerleaders (eg I'm here for you if you need me), and focus on doing their best; especially for their children.

IF THEY AREN'T TRAINED AS A BARBER, DON'T LET THEM CUT YOUR HAIR

SELF-CARE

Being a Child Protection Worker is often a thankless job, and those working alongside child welfare can sometimes feel the same. As with any helping profession, there is a risk of compassion fatigue as a mediator and especially as a Child Protection Mediator. The stories we hear are often very sad, generational, and traumatizing. As much as we would like to help everyone, and have everyone live in a perfect world, the mediator needs to be accepting of the fact that not everyone can be helped, not everyone wants to help themselves and sometimes, "good enough" has to do. Understanding these facts will go a long way towards self-care, as well as career longevity.

It doesn't matter if you are a worker, mediator, lawyer, judge, or collateral service provider, child welfare is emotional. It is a daunting profession in which you will see and experience many hardships. It can also be an incredibly fast-paced profession. If you are not able to manage and process your thoughts and feelings about the work, it will have a negative impact on you, on your family and friends, and on your clients.

When you struggle to process your feelings and it is having a negative impact on your life, you may be experiencing some form of compassion fatigue. Compassion fatigue is considered a short-term, negative response to secondary trauma based on the "helpers" repeated exposure to the client's descriptions of their own traumas. Symptoms include but are not limited to:

- difficulty concentrating
- intrusive imagery
- feeling hopeless
- exhaustion

- irritability

Vicarious trauma is somewhat different than compassion fatigue. Although vicarious trauma is also related to repeated exposure to another person's trauma, the helper's world view begins to shift. It has a more global, long-term impact on the helper as their fundamental beliefs begin to shift in a negative direction as a result of their experiences. It is a build-up of exposure to secondary trauma, and begins to elicit a trauma response in the clinician.

IF YOU DON'T TAKE CARE OF YOURSELF, YOU CAN'T TAKE CARE OF OTHERS

The focus of self-care should be on the promotion of mental wellness, and not on the prevention of mental illness. This helps us focus more on the desired outcome, and away from what we are trying to avoid. It is goal-directed thinking, and will be more successful as we strive to achieve something. If we constantly think "Don't do that," we become fixated on the negative action. This thought process fills us with more negative thoughts. Focus on what you want to achieve; mental wellness. This shift in thinking is also beneficial when working with clients. Work towards the goal. Remember the Nike commercials, and *Just Do It!*

THERAPY & PEER SUPPORT

Humans are social creatures by nature, so talking out our feelings can be a source of support. Sometimes by simply verbalizing what we are thinking and feeling, we gain a better understanding of what's happening inside. It's different to hear it than it is to just think it.

Therapy occurs with a trained professional in an emotionally safe place. There is no judgment! The therapist's role is to help you work through your thoughts and feelings in a healthy way. Although you may be focussed on a short-term, recent issue, the therapist will likely also focus on the long-term. They'll help you deal with the issue at hand, but also help you to plan for how you will deal with the same issue if it occurs in the future. Therapy is not simply about treating an issue. It is designed to help you understand your thoughts and feelings about an issue.

Again, focussing on mental wellness, therapy does not need to only occur in the bubble of negative thoughts and feelings. It can also be successful during emotionally healthy times. It can be preventative medicine. Much like people exercise to remain physically fit and prevent injury, therapy can be used as a way to maintain emotional health.

EVERY GOOD THERAPIST HAS A GOOD THERAPIST

Many TPA's have regular staff meetings and clinical supervision. These may be times when you can discuss troubling cases and feelings with other practitioners in the same field. There is a high probability that others will be struggling with the same feelings. Also, there is a chance that someone previously dealt with a similar case or situation. Although they are not you and cannot fully understand your thoughts and feelings, they may have some suggestions on how they managed the situation. Again, this should be a safe place to share your feelings and experiences but be aware of with whom you share. You want to be certain that the peers with whom you open up are positive supports.

PACE YOURSELF

It is important to know how many cases you can manage at one time. Clients deserve an efficient process and if things take too long (in their minds), they will begin to question your competence. Further, they will begin to contact you regularly for updates on the process. This will create added stress for you.

The mediator should also be very aware of the types of cases that they can manage. Managing ten civil mediations at one time is not the same as managing ten Family Mediations at one time. Managing ten CP Med's at one time is yet another type of challenge. The mediator again has a responsibility to themselves and to their clients to know how many files they can manage at one time in an efficient and effective manner.

WORK-LIFE BALANCE & BOUNDARIES

The topic of boundaries was discussed briefly in an earlier section of this book. Boundaries are critical to longevity in this profession. Many of our clients are in crisis, and need us a lot. Also, it is their life that often hangs in the balance. As a result, they do not shut it off. This leads to phone calls, emails, and text messages at all hours, and seven days per week. Although some mediators are good at not replying to those messages outside of working hours, the mediator will often think about their planned response. This may then have a negative impact on their family life. When outside of work, be outside of work in your mind as well. Effective strategies include, but are not limited to:

- a dedicated work phone that is shut down outside of business hours
- a dedicated work email address that is not checked outside of business hours

- a dedicated work computer that is shut down outside of office hours
- a post office box if you are a home-based business
- remind clients during intake appointments that messages will only be returned during business hours and if they have an emergency, they should contact their lawyer and/ or worker

Take time for yourself, and for your family. Being "on the clock" all of the time is not healthy. It's important to focus on your family when you are with them. Put your phone away, and BE with your family. When you're lying on your death bed, it is unlikely that you will wish that you had worked more.

EXERCISE

Much has been said about physical activity and mood. Along with the physical benefits of exercise, there are also emotional benefits of exercise. Many people reference the release of endorphins during exercise, but few actually understand what this actually means. Endorphins are released when pain impulses are triggered in the body. Physical activity is a form of trauma to the body (minor or major depending on the activity). The damaged tissue is repaired, and this creates physical changes in the body (ie why muscles look and function differently with ongoing exercise programs). Fortunately, the body typically releases more endorphins than it requires. So while the body is managing the current exercise "pain," it is also providing a state of relaxation after the fact.

MEDITATION/ YOGA

There are many benefits associated with meditation and yoga. Meditation emphasizes focussed breathing from a static position, whereas yoga is much like a moving meditation with periods of remaining in a static position. Although there is movement in yoga, the intent is for the movements to be calm, slow, and deliberate.

Research has shown that participation in meditation can increase grey matter in the brain, as well as increase gyrification in the brain. Gyrification is "folding" at the cerebral cortex, which may allow the brain to process information more quickly. There is also a correlation between meditation and lower blood pressure.

Benefits of meditation and yoga include, but are not limited to:
- improved learning and memory
- improved emotional regulation
- improved information processing
- improved memory recall
- improved attention
- improved flexibility (yoga-specific)
- reduced stress
- reduced depression
- reduced anxiety
- reduced risk of heart attack and stroke

LAUGH

Laughter is the best medicine! It is a release. It helps us cope with situations by giving attention to positive feelings and situations. Many people will use humour as a means of coping with difficult situations, and joking with colleagues can also give a sense of commonality. Be cautious however of your surroundings. Making an *inappropriate* joke or comment may be frowned upon by some clients, workers, lawyer, and other mediators.

Benefits of laughter include, but are not limited to:
- decreased stress hormones such as cortisol
- improved blood flow and circulation
- improved brain function and cognition
- improved mood
- increased pleasure hormones such as epinephrine and dopamine
- increased natural "painkiller" hormones such as endorphins
- increased release of antibody-producing cells
- reduces anxiety

CRY

If something is bothering you to the point where you feel like crying, then cry. These are called emotional tears for a reason. They are different than reflex tears and continuous tears. Allow yourself to be a human being with feelings. Keeping your feelings bottled up is not productive to you or to your clients. In fact, there is research to show that crying is good for you.

Psychiatrist Dr Judith Orloff describes tears as "your body's release valves for stress, sadness, grief, anxiety, and frustration." When a person cries, there are chemical reactions that occurs within the body. Analysis of emotional tears shows an increased level of hormones which are common in high stress situations. So, emotional tears are quite literally stress leaving the body. There is also research to show an increased level of endorphins in emotional tears which as discussed earlier, function to reduce physical pain. So by crying, stress leaves the body, and you will get natural pain relief; physically and emotionally.

As with laughter though, be sure to know your surroundings. Crying in a session with clients is not going to be productive, however crying around your peers should feel safe. It will also give your colleagues permission to allow themselves to emote if they feel the need.

WRITE

In his book on mental health awareness for families of first responders, Nick Halmasy writes "While reading can be relaxing, writing can be releasing." Writing our thoughts down can help us to review our actions, and the actions of others. Whether it be journaling or professional forums, writing can help us process our thoughts and feelings. In many ways, it can help us to move forward.

Writing can also be an effective tool to help others if the thoughts and feelings are shared. In fact, this book began out of frustration with how some mediators were not following the basics of the CP Med process. As a result, I started writing down my frustrations. Then, I started writing "an article." That article evolved into a multiple edition book that you're reading now. With hope, you have learned something from the contents so not only did writing help me process my feelings, it helped educate others as well.

FUNCTIONAL DEFINITIONS OF MEDIATION

'A' Not 'B'
'B' Not 'A'
Both 'A' and 'B'
Neither 'A' Nor 'B'

No two cases are exactly the same and what works in one situation, may not work in another. Sometimes "technique" A will work, but not B. Other times B will work, but not A. There are occasions when both A and B will work, and others where neither will work.

This emphasizes the mediator's need to stay current on research, and changing practices. We will never know it all but being open to new ideas, and an ability to think quickly, will help clients to resolve the issues at hand.

Assess
Adapt
Improvise

Identify
Assess
Manage

Never Say Never
Never Say Always

WHAT *NOT* TO DO

Book Joint Mediation Sessions Before All Intakes Completed

Booking joint mediation sessions before completing all of the intakes can give parties false hope. If the mediation then does not move forward, it can set up further conflict among the parties. An exception to this may be if there is a pending court date, and it is made VERY clear to ALL of the parties that there is still a chance that the mediation may not move forward based on the intakes of all parties. Further, a decision would not be provided until all of the parties have been met.

Disclose Content From An Intake Appointment

Information in a person's intake appointment is confidential; including the intake of CAS. It is not the mediator's role to explain to family members why CAS is involved or why CAS thinks mediation may be helpful. Sharing information from a participant's intake appointment may put people at risk of harm, or derail the mediation process. Some parties may become angry, especially if they learn that another party disclosed violence, control, or fear.

NARRATIVE:

A very experienced mediator friend, *Karl* has a very different philosophy on this topic. We routinely discuss this and honestly, I don't think we'll ever agree. *Karl* will get consent from CAS or family members to disclose information from intake appointments in an effort to decrease emotionality of subject matter at joint mediation session. I disagree with this but if you are to share any information from any intake appointments, consent is mandatory.

In an effort to protect yourself from liability, a signed, written consent is recommended.

Disclose Dates/ Times Of Intake Appointments

It is virtually impossible for a mediator to have every last bit of information. No matter how good a job the mediator does at screening, there always remains a risk that something is missed. As a result, dates and times of intake appointments (or arrival times in a shuttle mediation) should not be shared, because the mediator has no way of knowing exactly what actions another party may take.

Disclose Why Mediation Was Screened Out

Disclosing why a mediation file is screened out often feels like blame to one of the parties. If certain parties feel blamed for mediation not moving ahead, it may put others at risk or harm. Exceptions to this is if the mediator recommends another process. Then, the mediator may tell the parties of the suggested alternate method(s).

Facilitate Joint Mediation Session(s) Without CAS Present

An agent from CAS MUST be present for the joint mediation session. They are considered a party to the mediation. If CAS is not present, it is NOT a CP Med. As a result, MCYS should not be paying for the mediation.

Display Email Addresses Without Consent

Some clients do not want any of their personal information shared with the other parties. Doing so is a breach of their trust, and may put people at risk of harm. It is also best practice to ask about consent to display email addresses in a private conversation; not during a meeting with multiple parties.

Sign MOU

There is specific criteria required for a document to meet the threshold of a domestic contract. Signing a mediated agreement MAY meet that threshold, and create a legally binding document. The MOU should not be signed by the parties with the mediator, as there is an expectation that the parties will seek out Independent Legal Advice after the mediation. If the parties choose to sign the MOU, that is their prerogative. However, under no circumstances should the mediator sign the MOU as a witness.

Send MOU To Worker To Proof-Read And Approve

CAS is a party, just like all of the other parties to the mediation. Sending the MOU to them for approval or to proof-read demonstrates a lack of neutrality. If the mediator is not confident in their MOU-writing ability or would like their documentation proof-read, they should send it to a peer to review; not to a mediation party.

Start From A Paradigm Of CAS Supervisors Attending All Meetings

There are definitely times when it is necessary for the CAS supervisor to attend all meetings. Starting from this position however, is problematic. CAS has a tremendous amount of power, just by virtue of the legislation. In a typical CP Med (if there is such a thing), having a supervisor present can create further power imbalances. Family members often enter the process feeling marginalized, because they are "clients" sitting with "professionals." When a supervisor is added to the equation, it creates an additional layer of power for the CAS.

At times, it can also be disempowering to the worker. Once the family meets the supervisor, they may begin to bypass the worker for future case dialogue.

Supervisors are very much a part of the CP Med process, but more so in the background. Workers and supervisors need to have clear discussions during the mediation process, and a supervisor should be available for consultation if needed during a joint mediation session. Depending on the case dynamics however, they are rarely present for the joint mediation session.

Financial Mediation

Financial mediation takes special training, and is often best handled by a lawyer-mediator. Even "simple" financial mediations such as Child Support and Spousal Support have complicated impacts on an individual's financial situation. Unless the parties have had Independent Legal Advice, and have been given specific advice with respect to a financial mediation, parties should not engage in a financial mediation with anyone other than a lawyer-mediator.

There are also those who believe that financial issues are not a child protection matter. On the surface, this is true. Unfortunately, financial issues can fuel conflict exponentially. Adult conflict is definitely a child protection issue if it has a negative effect on the child.

If dealing with financial issues in a CP Med, they are best left until later in the process. Beyond the dollars and cents, the parties are more likely in need of discussion with respect to their parenting principles, communication, and conflict resolution strategies.

Rely Exclusively On Court Documents For Intake Information

There have been recent instances of CP mediators relying on court documentation exclusively for their intake information. This is completely unacceptable. When completing the intake process, the mediator is compelled to get their information from the parties; not from court documents. Although court documents may have some important information, there is no way to be certain that each party prepared their own documents. More often than not, the information contained in court documents has been prepared by a legal team; not the parties. Depending on the CAS, it may not even have been the worker who wrote their affidavits.

Most importantly, court documents are missing something critical; the human element. It is impossible to adequately screen for power imbalances and risk of violence based exclusively on words on paper. There must be conversations with the parties involved. The mediator must explore past experiences and if there is fear, the mediator has a responsibility to explore ways to design a safe process. If the documents outline a historic incident of abuse, there is no way of knowing that the victim remains fearful. Furthermore, there is no point of reference from the person responsible for the alleged maltreatment. Perhaps the story of abuse was completely made up. Conversely, the documents may not be up-to-date, and may be missing updated, critical developments such as a recent incident of violence or fear.

The court process is designed to fight. As a result, court documents are often written in a way to point out the flaws in others. The end results are documents filled with lists of negative attributes and experiences. Relying only on that negative information will not help the mediator move the parties forward. There is an obligation that the mediator have direct conversations with the parties to complete an accurate assessment of their experiences, and their mediation goals.

In most cases, the only legal documents that need to be reviewed as part of the intake process would be existing court orders, or legal separation agreements. This is so the mediator may better understand the legal parameters already in place. Relying exclusively on court documents for the mediator's intake process is negligent!

CONCLUSION

I hope that you have found this book useful, and informative. The information contained herein is not comprehensive. It is not everything. It is a starting point, and an additional resource. Although it is based on how I conduct CP Med, I have also done my best to highlight the strengths and pitfalls of other strategies.

Anyone considering CP Med should ensure that they read and understand the most recent version of the legislation relevant to their geographical area. Simply quoting statutes means nothing if you don't understand the implications of those words. Understanding the legislation, directives, and regulations in your area will also create more buy-in from workers, and the local Bar, and, help you navigate the process. You will then be better prepared to engage those involved, including family members.

Most importantly, I encourage you to remain focussed on providing a balanced process. Far too often, we get caught up in being "Service Providers." Yes, we are Service Providers, but we need to remember why we provide this service. The goal of mediation is to balance the equation, and make everyone feel like equals. It is to engage everyone, so that they may be the authors of their own plans. Getting buy-in from all of the clients, including families and CAS, will create better outcomes for children. That must remain at the forefront. If you fail to remain neutral and unbiased, you become yet another obstacle to overcome.

Finally, if you are new to Child Welfare, I highly recommend you complete an internship specific to CP Med, or shadow a Protection Worker for a few home visits. Although CP Med has its roots in Family Mediation, it is a different beast. Brace yourself!

Thanks for reading...

ARTICLES

STICKS & STONES
(October 5, 2012)

*"Sticks and Stones May Break My Bones
But Names Will Never Hurt Me"*

I think it's safe to say that just about every one of us has heard the above statement before. I also think that it's safe to say that the first time we heard it was probably from one of our parents. This phrase is typically expressed when a child complains of being called names in the school yard, or being picked on for being different. While our parents meant well by using this phrase, did they really understand what they were saying?

The truth of the matter is that the title phrase is elementary. While it outlines the risks of physical injury, it does not acknowledge the complexity of emotional wounds. It also implies that physical injury is more concerning than emotional injury.

In general, most physical injuries can be seen; especially when we're talking about the effects of being in contact with sticks and stones. Furthermore, physical injuries sustained from such an event are generally easily treatable. Emotional injuries however, are quite different. They may include depression, aggression, sadness, or even lack of any reaction. Let's take a closer look.

Yes, it is true that sticks and stones may break my bones. As a child, I fell and broke my wrist. While at car accidents as a firefighter, I have seen many people with cuts and broken bones. During my work in child welfare, I was involved in a case where a three year old child was severely burned on his forearm by his caregiver. It was never made clear if the burn was intentional, but he also had several bruises on his body in various locations. All of these examples clearly detail physical injury.

With all of the examples listed above, the physical treatment is straight-forward. For the broken bones, have them reset and put a cast on the limb. The cuts may require stitches. After a week, the stitches are removed and the patient may keep a visible scar. For the burned child, he was removed from the caregiver's home, and the burn treated. He was left with a scar on the posterior of his forearm and hand. In each case, the individual was able to carry on a normal life after the physical injury healed.

Now, let's look at "Names will never hurt me." Bullying, failed relationships, uncertainty of sexuality, abuse (verbal, physical, emotional, sexual), and lack of emotional support may all lead to the same thing; emotional injury. There are many other examples, but these few help to highlight my point. Perhaps the greatest contributor to long-term emotional injury is lack of emotional support.

Each and every one of us has had situations in our life that have been upsetting. Some people carry the burden of that upset, while others find ways to let it go. If we do not develop ways to cope with emotional injury, we are left with emotional scars. Unlike the healed cut or broken bone, these scars are not easily visible to the naked eye, and require advanced technology to be seen at all in some chronic cases. We may see some outward signs of mental health difficulties such as violence, excessive crying, or mania, but there are many people with emotional wounds that we would never know about.

Think of how many people die by suicide, but their outward signs of depression were not noticed. They are often described as shy, introverted or different. Their withdrawn presentation may have been a sign but because it was not exceptionally different, it was not paid attention to. Then there are cases of murder by prominent members of the community followed by comments of "Such a nice boy." The deaths are an outward sign, but often noticed too late.

While every case of emotional injury does not lead to physical death, it may lead to some form of emotional death. Examples may include fear of commitment, being emotionally guarded, promiscuity, risk-taking, or addictions. Many people use some or all of the above to help mask the emotional wounds that they have and as a result, they miss out on possibly wonderful opportunities.

These incidents occur because of emotional injuries that have not been addressed by the person experiencing them. It's not accurate to say that the injuries are healed but rather, we learn to re-evaluate their meaningfulness in our lives. Left untreated, these injuries may begin to manifest themselves through behaviour issues, learning disabilities, suicide and more. In medicine, treatment implies a passive process. While some emotional injuries may be treated with medication, most often involve a much more active process. There are many avenues to explore but ultimately, the answer lies within the person who has been wounded.

As human beings, we must all do our best to help others develop the necessary tools of tolerance, compassion, and understanding. With this foundation, people will be more apt to seek assistance when they need it. They will also be more inclined to speak out against someone else being emotionally harmed. Whether a child or an adult, we all have a responsibility to help others, and to speak out against emotional harm. As family and friends, our role is not to tell people "I told you so" when they fall or feel down. Our role is to help them up, and tell them that we're there for them. That's the support they need.

FILLING THE VOID
(February 25, 2014)

For years, there has been discussion about *The Void* in martial arts. Much of what we study relates to filling the void during physical interaction. Once there has been physical contact between two people during a physical interaction, they become one physical entity. When contact is broken, a void is created between the previous points of contact. During much of my journey, I was under the impression that I needed to fill the void before my partner in order to dominate the situation. I was wrong!

I finally began to understand the concept of *Filling the Void* about one month ago; eleven months after my father died and over twenty-two years after I began martial arts training. The light bulb went off while in a counselling session when I was discussing the loss of my father. Yet another example of how the true study of martial arts is beyond the mats, and not just about physical drills.

During the conversation with my counsellor, I began to parallel physical interaction with relationships. When we care about someone, we create an emotional connection. This connection is similar to physical connection in the attacker-defender drills. When one of the people in the relationship is no longer present (break-up, death, personality change etc), a void is created. Once the void has been created, it needs to be filled. If it is not filled, the space remains empty. When thinking of the physical interaction, if the void is created and nobody moves to fill it, you're both stuck in place. The same happens in emotional relationships.

My father and I were incredibly close. I considered him my best friend, and we never struggled to find conversation. When he died, I was devastated. I had lost my best friend, my role model, my hero. This created a huge void in my life, and lots of intense, internal struggle.

My father died of cancer. He was diagnosed nine years before he died and really, he was pretty healthy for most of that time. As he got more ill, I found myself helping out more around my parents' home. When he finally died, I found myself taking on all of the maintenance responsibilities of their home, and also trying to be all things for my mother.

This created lots of internal conflict, because I was attempting to fill the void by being him. In some strange way, I was attempting to keep him alive by taking on his responsibilities. It was no longer a case of a child doing more for aging parents. It was me imposing myself as a surrogate. What made it even more difficult was that because I was so focussed on subconsciously keeping him alive, I was not working through my own grief.

Now, the void created by his death still needs to be filled. The question is with what intent. I've been filling the void, but in a very unhealthy manner. Now, I need to fill the void in a functional and healthy way. The way I'm doing this is by setting boundaries on my various roles in my personal life. Also when doing things my father normally would have done, I ask myself if I'm doing it to be him, to be like him, or to be the grown child of an aging parent. I also try to focus on positive memories, and lessons learned from my father. All of these things help me to fill the void in a healthier, more functional way.

Now, back to the mats and our martial arts scenario. Someone has thrown a strike at you, and you've redirected them. In your redirection, your hand had contact with their shoulder, but your hand came away from the shoulder. You have also taken your partner from a place of balance to a place of imbalance. Several voids have been created, and those spaces need to be filled.

If you think that you must fill the void before your partner, you are more than likely filling the void in a destructive way. The goal is simply to be first which means you win, and they lose. If the partner moves first in an attempt to fill the void and you adjust to simply cause them harm/ imbalance, you've also entered into a destructive space.

The dilemma becomes intent. We must take into consideration why the void needs to be filled. What is the motivation? Is your partner filling the void to counter, or are they simply adjusting to retreat. If you harm someone who's trying to retreat, you've then become the negative in the interaction. Of course, it goes the other way too. Perhaps your motivation for filling the void is one of distance or retreat. If the idea is to neutralize and not destroy, the intent is positive.

When it comes to the voids in your life, you need to continually ask yourself what, why, and how. What is the void? Why am I trying to fill the void, and how am I going to fill the void in a healthy and functional way. Filling it blindly or ignoring it will create a state of imbalance both physically and emotionally.

THE FAMILY TRIANGLE
Using Geometry to Move Families Forward
January 24, 2017

Mediation is designed to assist people with working out differences, so that they are able to function better as parents while living separately. *The Family Triangle* is an effective tool in helping families shift their focus from the past to the present, and ultimately, to the future. While family relationships are complex, *The Family Triangle* provides a simplistic representation of the child-parent-parent relationship.

The concept of *The Family Triangle* is just that; a simple triangle. One point represents the child, and one point represents each parent. Further, the points are connected. In genealogy, the child would generally be seen at the bottom of the diagram. With *The Family Triangle*, the child is at the top. Visualizing the triangle in this way allows people to view the relationship from a structural perspective. There is a base (a foundation), a distinct top (a purpose), and everyone is connected.

Figure 1:

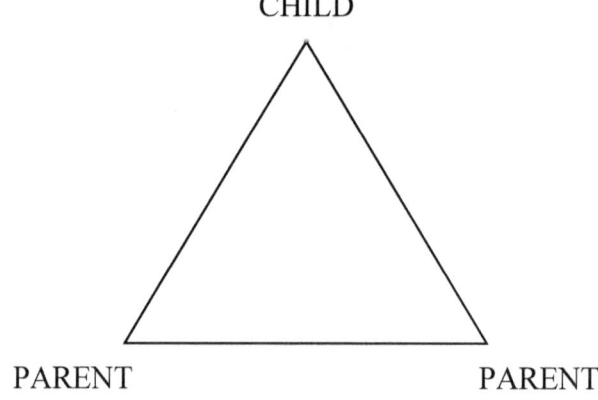

This makes it easier for people to understand the concept, and helps create change in their parenting relationship. Unlike the typical family hierarchy, this image more closely parallels the dynamics in a family group. There is a strong base at the bottom, with an apex reaching for the sky. If children are told "The Sky Is The Limit," parents have an obligation to help the child reach for that goal. This is accomplished by working cooperatively, and providing the child with the necessary foundation.

Communication

The Family Triangle illustrates basic connections that must exist in a child-parent group. While all of the lines are important, in mediation, special focus is often needed on the connection between the parents. From a functional perspective, it represents communication, understanding of differences, and support of each other. It is also acknowledging that even though the romantic relationship ended, the parental relationship must continue. It is genuinely putting the needs of the child above of the wants and needs of the parents.

As shown in Figure 1, *The Family Triangle* has the child at the top with the parents as the base. As children age, they become physically bigger and heavier. Over time, their emotional weight also increases. This is especially true for families engaged in mediation. Think of a child starting their emotional journey with a pencil case and by the time they're a teenager, they may already be carrying a suitcase of emotional baggage. Parents are often left unprepared.

As the base of *The Family Triangle*, the parents remain as the support for the child; constantly trying to prop them up and help them reach their goals. The dilemma is that without functional and productive communication between the parents, there is nothing keeping the child's base points connected and secure. Over time, with lack of communication and lack of understanding, the base points slide further and further apart. Eventually, the base can no longer support the peak, and the child emotionally crashes to the ground.

Figure 2:

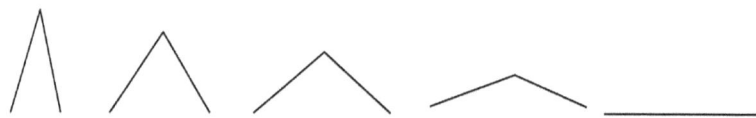

It is through this simple illustration that many parents come to a realization about their family group. To keep the base from sliding apart and the child from crashing, parents need to maintain functional and productive communication with each other. They do not need to be in constant communication, but they need to demonstrate an ability to communicate effectively to show the child they are working together in the child's best interests.

Parenting Styles

The Family Triangle can also be used to discuss healthy parenting styles, and the need for balance. Many clients express how the other parent has a different parenting style from them, and this causes great stress. The triangle allows clients to visualize the need for similarities and differences in their parenting.

It is important for parents to have some similarities in their parenting style, but they do not need to be identical. In fact, even in-tact families have parents with some differences in parenting styles. Variation is good! The slight variations in dealing with day-to-day issues help the child to adjust to variations they will encounter in the outside world. Using *The Family Triangle* demonstrates that if the styles are too similar, the base is too narrow. The structure is unstable and even though the child's emotional weight may not be as high, it takes less to emotionally knock the child over.

Figure 3:

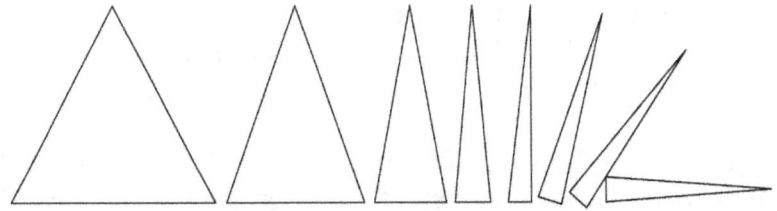

Conversely, if the parenting styles are too different, this again increases the emotional weight of the child on an unsteady base. The child then lives in a world of chaos, because the differences far outnumber the similarities. As in Figure 2, the base slips out and once again, the child emotionally crumbles to the ground.

Conclusion

Clinicians are often looking for new, intricate ways of interacting with clients. Far too often however, the processes and strategies become complicated and confusing. Sometimes, the best teaching tools are the simplest teaching tools. Clients engaged in the mediation process are often emotionally drained by the time they enter into the process. By using a simple geometric shape, the message gets through without creating further stress or confusion.

Article edited by: Dr Michael A Heintz & Nick Halmasy, HonBA, MACP

DEBRIEF & GRIEVE
September 22, 2017

Today as I sat at the back of the room, the emotions returned. It was during a workshop with respect to mental health awareness for first responders. Although "retired" for the last three years, I had been a volunteer firefighter for almost ten years before that. As I listened to the speakers share their stories, one speaker in particular tripped a switch in me.

Suddenly, it was July 6, 2006 at 4am, and I was back in that family's home. I was doing chest compressions for the very first time, in a zone of uncertainty, and hearing the 82 year old woman's son going hysterical in the background. Although we did our best, the woman died at the scene.

There were three firefighters on the truck for that call; a Captain, a Lieutenant, and an inexperienced firefighter; me. On the way back to the fire hall, the Lieutenant glanced at me in the rear-view mirror and said "You ok with that, Paul?" I simply said "Ya," and continued my gaze out of the window in the backseat of the fire truck.

Not only was it my first time doing compressions, but it also involved a mother and a son. That held a special dynamic for me, because of my personal relationships. At the time though, I never let on about how bothered I was by that call. It happened in a time and place where feelings were not discussed. The fire service and farming community in which I lived were clubs for hard "Men;" not sissies who talked about their feelings. For the era, "You ok with that, Paul?" was actually stepping out of the box. Unfortunately, that was the extent of the debrief.

Fast-forward to today. I was in a room filled with first responders, mental health professionals, victims services, and survivors of incredibly difficult situations. In spite of all of that, I still felt the need to stifle my feelings and tears when listening to some of the speakers. In the realm of those in the helping professions, there should have been no safer place than that to allow myself to emote. Yet, I didn't.

I worried about stigma. I worried about drawing attention to myself. Would my friends make negative comments that I was soft or over-sensitive? Although I know the uncomfortable comments would come from a place of ignorance and lack of awareness, I also knew that they would hurt.

So, here I am processing my feelings to myself almost twelve hours later. During the workshop however, I made a point of paying special attention to how I felt in that moment: a skill taught to me by my therapist. I then wrote out my feelings because by acknowledging them, I can start to accept them.

So, in that moment, I felt tremendous anxiety. It felt like my heart was skipping beats and racing. There was tension in my neck, and a lump in my throat. I felt like I could wail at any time, and I was trapped. Trapped in that room, trapped in my body, and trapped in my mind.

I also felt incredible sadness. Sadness that I would not allow myself to publically cry, and sadness that I had not thought about that family for years. Their lives were forever changed and even though it was a milestone call for me, it eventually just became another day at the office.

I have spent the entire day engulfed with anxiety and sadness, yet I have still not allowed myself to weep and feel those feelings. I have taken the first step by expressing these thoughts and feelings here. The second step will be to share them. Only by sharing them can I begin the path to discovery and recovery. Only by sharing them can someone know that I need help; even if only for a moment.

Although I am no longer a firefighter, I remain connected with emergency services. Also as a family professional, I am constantly told stories of trauma and sadness. The feelings I experienced today are likely to come again with other stories. The secret is to discuss them, and the feelings. Share the stories, and share the feelings. The content of the story isn't as important as the affect of the story. Allow yourself to debrief and grieve. It will help you to move forward...

LETTERS

Rochelle MacCarthy, Child Protection Worker

I have been employed in the field of child protection for almost 17 years.

Our work tends to result in a reactive response to challenges experienced by families.

Child protection mediation is one process that attempts to shift the reactive response to one that is potentially pro-active. Families are offered an opportunity to work together to create a plan, hopefully prior to any harm being experienced by the involved child(ren).

Exposure to parental conflict as the result of separation and/or custody and access issues has the potential to cause harm, especially emotional harm, to the child (ren). When an individual is hurt and not feeling heard, they may respond in a defensive manner or with anger. At times, the parents, when so overwhelmed with their own issues, forget how the drama and conflict may be impacting their child(ren). The child(ren), as a result, end up caught in the crossfire of two angry and hurt parents.

Child protection mediation empowers people to participate in the creation of a functional co-parenting plan. Such a plan has the potential to provide a child with a peaceful and loving existence with both parents rather than live with stress, confusion and possible fear.

I have and will continue to utilize child protection mediation. I have seen successes and partial successes with families who use mediation. On occasion it has not worked out. The parents were not yet ready to move past their own issues in order to best meet the needs of their children. Even in these cases, involvement with child protection mediation may have helped plant the seed; start the thought process, of what these caregivers need to do to move forward, make change and decrease risk of harm to their child (ren).

Carolyn McAlpine - Child Protection Mediator, Family Group Coordinator

After being a Child Protection Mediator for 12 years, I have seen many changes take place in CAS structures across Ontario. As a result, I have watched many new workers adjust to their very difficult roles, and worked with many families as they navigate a system that can seem daunting and overwhelming. It has been encouraging to watch the gradual understanding and belief that for families involved with CAS, going to court should be the last choice.

Although CAS workers can have a bad "rep", I have experienced many who care deeply for the families with whom they work. They also welcome the opportunity to work with a neutral person who isn't there to take anyone's side, but to provide a structure where everyone's voice is heard, and each person has a say in crafting an agreement that will address the child protection concerns.

From the family's perspective, CPM allows them an opportunity to express their concerns and hopes in a safe, confidential process. Families have expressed relief and gratitude as their voices are heard, and their ideas are incorporated into an Agreement that allows them to feel less overwhelmed. They also gain some hope and ability to move forward in their lives. Many families have been open to learning different ways of communicating, and understanding their children's needs. This helps them hear the concerns in a way that isn't attacking, but in an attempt to help them reach their full potential.

When Child Protection Mediation works, everyone involved has a hand in developing a more personal and acceptable plan that addresses everyone's concerns, in a way that feels more acceptable and provides more buy-in from the family.

Of course, CPM isn't always successful or able to be used. When there is active mental health and/ or addictions, or severe domestic violence that could put a family member at immediate risk of harm, there is less chance of a sustainable, safe agreement. With that being said, we have learned over the years that even the most difficult situations can gain something from the process.

I worry that in an extremely busy and often seemingly endless stream of work for the CAS workers and Supervisors, the number of CPM referrals made will decrease, limiting the opportunities for families to experience a very beneficial alternative to court. I am however, very hopeful that everyone will continue to see the value in using CPM and it will continue to be used as a first and prioritized process.

Stefanie Rudd, Family & Child Protection Lawyer

As a lawyer that represents parents in Child Protection proceedings, I am always looking for ways to level the playing field between my client and CAS. Clients are often very distrustful of the child welfare system in general, and many have had experiences that justify their perspective. They can be reluctant to engage with their worker or even hostile, even if the client is in a relatively strong position and it would be in their best interests to be cooperative.

Child protection mediation has the advantage of being facilitated by a neutral third party and it is "Closed." So, in theory, it is a mechanism for my client to participate in a direct and meaningful way without feeling afraid of saying the wrong thing, or worried that the worker will misrepresent what they said. Without a neutral third party and the security of confidentiality, it is unlikely that a full and frank discussion of the issues and possible resolutions would be possible.

I offer this as a suggestion for all aspiring Family and Child Protection Mediators. If a family member is represented by a lawyer, it would be helpful if the mediator informed the lawyer that the file has been referred for mediation. CAS communicates with parties directly and it is not unusual for them to make arrangements without keeping us in the loop. If I had my way, I would like a few minutes to chat with the mediator to confirm the issues that are being mediated, as well as the approximate timeline for mediation. This allows me to remain up-to-date on what is happening, and I am then better able to support my clients during that process, and through their child welfare experience.

Shannon Sawa, Child Protection Worker

Having over a decade of experience as a child protection worker, I have seen the system go through many changes that have impacted the way I have been able to deliver services and support families. While some directives and services have not transferred well from policy to practice, the introduction of child protection mediation has, in my opinion, been a much-needed addition to an already limited list of useful alternatives in the field. When files had reached an 'impasse', there were few options available to front line workers to work through the issues and challenges. This ultimately resulted in many files closing that should have remained open, or CAS taking families to court.

Both options I mention almost always resulted in increased tension and conflict, and loss of trust and effective communication between workers and families. This ultimately made children more vulnerable. In my experience, it became a perpetual cycle of conflict that rarely resulted in the successful resolution of child protection concerns.

When CPM was introduced however, it offered a means to break the cycle. That is not to say that CPM works every time it used, but it does offer CAS' and families, children/youth and communities an alternate child-focused and inclusive process to engage in. It allows all parties to participate in a non-threatening, voluntary, flexible, creative and anti-oppressive service that is delivered by trained mediators. This often results in the neutralization of the power imbalances that exist between CAS and families. When these barriers are lowered or at least addressed, there is greater opportunity for meaningful change. Aside from being a task-focused process, it also fosters emotional healing and trust re-building, by allowing parties to engage in open and safe communication about the long-standing issues, preventing the parties from moving forward.

This process cannot be successful without a you! The mediator! The common denominator in all of my success stories with CPM have been how the mediator used their skills and knowledge to successfully navigate and support families, youth, and child protection workers through the process. From start to finish, the mediator is the one who guides the process, manages and balances emotions, checks boundaries, and keeps parties on task and focused. It is very easy for mediators to lose perspective due to the level of emotion being carried so be mindful, be present and engage in critical self-reflection often!

Good luck!

THANK YOU

1st EDITION:

I would like to thank the following people who have helped with this project on some level. Some of them proof-read early drafts, provided suggestions, or helped with topics and design. Others have helped shape me as a mediator either directly or indirectly...

- Rob Burriss
- Paul Hamilton
- Paul Lamain
- Hilary Linton
- Jared Phillips
- Jess Uddenberg
- Nick Halmasy
- Dr Michael Heintz
- Carolyn Leach
- Carolyn McAlpine
- David Tonge
- Vicky Visca

2nd EDITION:

In addition to those thanked in the first edition, I would also like to thank:

- Maryann King
- Kattie Ross
- Shannon Sawa
- Rochelle MacCarthy
- Stephanie Rudd

and as always, my amazing wife and children...

PJB

APPENDIX

PJB

Appendix A:

| CONSENT TO DISCLOSE INFORMATION |

I _____ of _____
  (Name of Parent/Guardian or Child over 12 Years)   (Address)

authorize _____ to release information (including file history, family
              (name of child welfare agency)
history, & contact information) pertaining to myself and my children,

    Name: _____   DOB: _____

    Name: _____   DOB: _____

    Name: _____   DOB: _____

    Name: _____   DOB: _____

    Name: _____   DOB: _____

to:

Mediation Agency	Transfer Payment Agency	Office of the Children's Lawyer
Address	Address	393 University Ave
AND	AND	14th Floor
		Toronto, ON
		M5W 1W9

for the purpose of Child Protection Mediation and/ or Family Group Decision Making.

This consent will remain in effect from _____ to _____.
                                          (Date)   (Date)

My signature means that:
1. I have read this consent or have had this consent read to me. I understand and agree to its contents.
2. I have been informed that I may cancel my consent by giving a written statement to the Facilitator and/ or my Child Protection Worker at any time.

Signed _____ on _____
         (Parent/Guardian or Child over 12)   (Date)

Witness: _____ Signature _____
                      (Name)

Guide To Child Protection Mediation

Appendix B:

 Ontario Ministry of Children and Youth Services

Notice: Where Alternative Dispute Resolution is Proposed Under the *Child and Family Services Act*

Please fax the form to the address below:

Office of the Children's Lawyer
Ministry of the Attorney-General
393 University Avenue, 14th Floor
Toronto ON M5G 1W9
Tel: 416 314-8062
Fax: 416 314-8050
Attn.: ADR Intake Co-ordinator

Section I Child Information

Last Name	First Name	Date of Birth (yyyy/mm/dd)	Is the child a minor parent? ☐ Yes ☐ No
Last Name	First Name	Date of Birth (yyyy/mm/dd)	Is the child a minor parent? ☐ Yes ☐ No
Last Name	First Name	Date of Birth (yyyy/mm/dd)	Is the child a minor parent? ☐ Yes ☐ No
Last Name	First Name	Date of Birth (yyyy/mm/dd)	Is the child a minor parent? ☐ Yes ☐ No

Section II Contact Information

1. Children's Aid Society

Name of Agency

Name of Child Protection Worker

Address (Number and Street)		Suite/Unit/Apt.	City/Town
Province	Postal Code	Telephone Number (inc. area code) ( )	Fax Number (inc. area code) ( )
Name of Lawyer			Lawyer's Telephone Number (inc. area code) ( )

2. Parents/Caregivers

Last Name	First Name	Relationship to Child
Address (Number and Street)		Suite/Unit/Apt.
City/Town	Province	Postal Code	Telephone Number (inc. area code) ( )
Name of Lawyer			Lawyer's Telephone Number (inc. area code) ( )

Do any of the children reside at the parent/caregiver's address?
☐ Yes ☐ No If "Yes," please provide name(s) of child(ren):

PJB

Last Name	First Name		Relationship to Child
Address (Number and Street)			Suite/Unit/Apt.
City/Town	Province	Postal Code	Telephone Number (inc. area code) ( )
Name of Lawyer			Lawyer's Telephone Number (inc. area code) ( )

Do any of the children reside at the parent/caregiver's address?
☐ Yes ☐ No   If "Yes," please provide name(s) of child(ren):

3. Other Participants, if known

Last Name	First Name		Relationship to Child
Address (Number and Street)			Suite/Unit/Apt.
City/Town	Province	Postal Code	Telephone Number (inc. area code) ( )
Name of Lawyer			Lawyer's Telephone Number (inc. area code) ( )

Do any of the children reside at this participant's address?
☐ Yes ☐ No   If "Yes," please provide name(s) of child(ren):

Last Name	First Name		Relationship to Child
Address (Number and Street)			Suite/Unit/Apt.
City/Town	Province	Postal Code	Telephone Number (inc. area code) ( )
Name of Lawyer			Lawyer's Telephone Number (inc. area code) ( )

Do any of the children reside at this participant's address?
☐ Yes ☐ No   If "Yes," please provide name(s) of child(ren):

4. Language
Does this family require services in French?
☐ Yes ☐ No

Section III   Issues Proposed for ADR
Is ADR proposed:
- in relation to a child/children who are or may be in need of protection?
  ☐ Yes ☐ No   If "Yes," proceed to Part 1 of this section.
- in relation to an openness order?
  ☐ Yes ☐ No   If "Yes," proceed to Part 2 of this section.

208

Guide To Child Protection Mediation

Part 1 Matters relating to children who are or may be in need of protection

Is there an ongoing court proceeding in relation to this matter?
☐ Yes ☐ No

Provide brief description of protection concerns

_____
_____
_____
_____

What are the issues proposed for ADR?

☐ Parent/teen conflict
☐ Expiring temporary care agreement
☐ Placement issues
☐ Terms of supervision orders
☐ Access issues
☐ Crown wardship orders/reviews
☐ Foster parents/CAS/parent issues
☐ Long term care issues
☐ Poor communication between worker and parents
☐ Length of time in care and conditions for return
☐ Other *(Please specify)* _____

Part 2 Matters in relation to openness orders

Please attach a copy of the openness order.

Is a
☐ variation of the openness order, or
☐ termination of the openness order
being sought?

Who has applied to vary or terminate the openness order?
_____

Was the application brought
☐ before adoption, or
☐ after adoption?

What are the proposed issues for ADR?
_____
_____
_____
_____

209

PJB

Section IV Criminal Matters

Have any charges been laid in relation to this matter?
☐ Yes ☐ No

Are there any pending criminal investigations in relation to this matter?
☐ Yes ☐ No

Have criminal record checks been requested for any of the parents/caregivers/participants?
☐ Yes ☐ No

Section V ADR Process

What prescribed method of ADR is proposed?

☐ Child protection mediation
☐ Family group conferencing
☐ Aboriginal approach
☐ Other *(Please specify)* _____
☐ Not yet known

Has a mediator/facilitator been chosen?
☐ Yes ☐ No

Name of Mediator/Facilitator	Telephone Number *(inc. area code)* ( )

Section VI Optional Information

Please provide any other information that may be material to the intake process at the Office of the Children's Lawyer.
(for example: child's special needs, any issues that may impact on child's ability to communicate, any language barriers)

_____

_____

Section VII Signature

In the opinion of this worker:
☐ there is no immediate risk to the child(ren)'s safety; and
☐ the proposed participants have the capacity to participate in an ADR process.

Last Name	First Name

Position	Telephone Number *(inc. area code)* ( )

Signature _____   Date *(yyyy/mm/dd)* _____

210

Appendix C:

CONFIDENTIALITY AGREEMENT

(Mediation Intake)

1. Mediation is a voluntary process, and any participant has the right to withdraw from the process at any time.

2. The mediator was an employee of the Hastings Children's Aid Society until July 4, 2011. The mediator is no longer an employee of the Hastings Children's Aid Society and as such, does not have access to the family's child welfare history beyond what is disclosed in the mediation process.

3. The mediator will not voluntarily disclose any verbal and/ or written communication that takes place during this meeting. The following exceptions apply:
   - Disclosure for my lawyer or third party advisors;
   - Where information suggests an actual or perceived threat to human life and/ or safety (notify CAS for a child, notify Police for an adult);
   - Where ordered to do so by law;
   - Research and/ or educational purposes (non-identifying information);
   - On written consent

4. I consent to the presence of language interpreters, mediation interns and/ or assistants for the purposes of professional training. All such observers and/ or participants are also bound by the same rules of confidentiality as the mediator as outlined in Paragraph 3.

5. I shall not record the content of any mediation appointments through any means such as audio, video etc.

6. I shall not summons nor otherwise require the mediator to testify and/or produce records and/ or notes in any current or future civil proceedings.

I acknowledge that I have read the *Confidentiality Agreement* or had it read to me, and understand this agreement.

Name (Print)	Signature	Date
Name (Print)	Signature	Date
Third Party as Per Paragraph 3	Signature	Date
	Signature	Date

Appendix D:

INTAKE

1st Nations: ☐ Yes ☐ No **Band:** _____ **Children:** _____

Lawyer: ☐ Yes ☐ No **Name:** _____ **Interview Children:** ☐ Yes ☐ No
OK to Call: ☐ Yes ☐ No
Court: ☐ None   ☐ CFSA   ☐ Family   **Next:** _____ **Restrictions:** ☐ Yes ☐ No

History: _____

_____
_____
_____
_____
_____
_____
_____
_____
_____
_____
_____
_____
_____
_____
_____
_____
_____
_____
_____
_____
_____

MH: _____

Adds: _____

Strengths: _____

Goals: _____

Preferred Appointment Time: _____   **Same Room:** ☐ Yes ☐ No

Appendix E:

INTAKE - Worker

Court: ☐ None ☐ CFSA ☐ Family **Next:** _____ **Restrictions:** ☐ Yes ☐ No
OCL Notified: ☐ Yes ☐ No **Assigned:** ☐ Yes ☐ No
OCL Name: _____
1st Nations: ☐ Yes ☐ No **Band:** _____
Children: **Interview Children:** ☐ Yes ☐ No

History: _____

_____

MH: _____

Adds: _____

Strengths: _____

Goals: _____

Preferred Appointment Time: **Same Room:** ☐ Yes ☐ No

PJB

Appendix F:

CLOSING LETTER

Date

Worker
c/o Children's Aid Society
123 CAS Lane
Your City, ON
1A2 B3C

Sent via email

Re: Family Name Mediation

Dear Worker:

This letter is to inform you that the above matter is not proceeding at this time. Given this was a Child Protection Mediation as defined in the Ministry of Children & Youth Services Policy Directive CW 005-06, it was a closed process. I am not able to disclose the reason(s) why mediation was terminated. This includes to family members, judges, lawyers and/ or the worker(s). This is not however, a reflection on any one person, and file closure should not be used against any of the parties.

Should you require more information, please don't hesitate to contact me.

Sincerely:

Appendix G:

AGREEMENT TO MEDIATE

This is an Agreement Between:

_____

and _____

and _____

and _____

and _____

and _____

and _____

("the parties")

AND

"THE MEDIATOR"
(Name of Mediator)

1. The people named above want to try to settle the dispute between them through mediation with "The Mediator."

2. <u>Role of Mediator</u>
   Each person understands that the mediator does not represent any of the parties, and is not acting as a lawyer (whether trained as one or not) for any of them. The mediator's job is to help the parties to come to an agreement which the parties think is fair and reasonable, and in the best interests of the child(ren).

3. Independent Legal Representation
   The parties understand that the mediator will not give them legal advice or a legal opinion. The parties understand that they can and should speak to a lawyer about their situation, and that they can do so at any time.

4. Confidentiality
   The parties agree that mediation is confidential with the following exceptions:
   a) The mediator can talk or write about the case without using identifying information for research of educational purposes;
   b) The mediator must report any suspicions that a child may be in need of protection under The Child and Family Services Act.
   c) The mediator must disclose where there are reasonable grounds to believe that there is a real or perceived threat to any person's life or physical safety.
   d) The mediator may speak to a third party where an individual consents to the disclosure of his or her own personal information.
   e) The terms of an agreement, memorandum of understanding or plan arising from the mediation can be shared with the court, and all counsel, including counsel for the child where applicable.
   f) Participants may always discuss the content of Mediation with their lawyer.

The parties agree that neither the participants nor the mediator can be subpoenaed, required to testify or called to give evidence relating to representations, statements or admissions made in the course of the mediation, or to produce or called to produce documents prepared or exchanged during the mediation in a civil proceeding.

No parties, including their lawyers, shall take any notes or recordings of any joint mediation session(s). The only exception to this rule is with respect to a lawyer representing a child when the child is not in attendance for the joint mediation session(s). Notes taken by a child's lawyer shall only contain a list of agreements reached in principle.

5. Bringing Other People into the Mediation
The mediator may ask other people to participate in the mediation if the parties agree.

6. Disclosure of Information
The parties agree that they will each make available any information that may help to resolve the dispute.

7. Mediation Sessions
The mediator will schedule the time and place of the mediation sessions with the parties. The parties agree to give the mediator 24 hours notice if the session has to be cancelled.

The mediator may meet with the parties together or individually.

8. Conclusion of Mediation
Any party has the right to withdraw from the mediation at any time. The mediator has the right to end or suspend the mediation where continuing the process could harm or prejudice one or more of the parties or the child(ren).

The only information the mediator will send to the parties and their lawyer(s) will be a list of any agreements in principle reached. No agreements reached in mediation are binding and it is strongly recommended that they be reviewed by each participant's counsel.

9. Further Agreements
The parties agree that none of them will begin any court action during the course of mediation without first advising the other party/parties and the mediator. Any court action already started will be adjourned until the mediation ends.

The parties agree that they have read this agreement or had this agreement read to them, understand it, and agree to take part in mediation on the basis of this agreement.

_____day of _____20____

―――――――――――――――――――
Signature

―――――――――――――――――――
Signature

―――――――――――――――――――
Signature

―――――――――――――――――――
Signature

―――――――――――――――――――
Signature

―――――――――――――――――――
Signature

―――――――――――――――――――
Mediator

Appendix G:

IMPORTANT FAMILY LAW FACTS

Below is a list of important Family Laws Facts that I often reference during a mediation process.

ARBITRATION ACT (S.O. 1991):

s.5(3) Oral agreements – An arbitration agreement need not be in writing.

s.11(1) Duty of arbitrator – An arbitrator shall be independent of the parties and shall act impartially.

s.12 No revocation – A party may not revoke the appointment of an arbitrator.

s.13(1) Challenge – A party may challenge an arbitrator only on one of the following grounds:

1. Circumstances exist that may give rise to a reasonable apprehension of bias.
2. The arbitrator does not possess qualifications that the parties have agreed are necessary.

s.17(1) Arbitral tribunal may rule on its own jurisdiction – An arbitral tribunal may rule on its own jurisdiction to conduct the arbitration and may in that connection rule on objections with respect to the existence or validity of the arbitration agreement.

s.50.1 Family arbitration awards – Family arbitration awards are enforceable only under the Family Law Act.

CHILD, YOUTH & FAMILY SERVICES ACT (CYFSA, R.S.O. 2017):

s.17(1) Resolution of issues by prescribed method of alternative dispute resolution – If a child is or may be in need of protection under this Act, a society shall consider whether a prescribed method of alternative dispute resolution could assist in resolving any issue related to the child or a plan for the child's care..

s.125(1) Duty to report child in need of protection – Despite the provisions of any other Act, if a person, including a person who performs professional or official duties with respect to children, has reasonable grounds to suspect one of the following, the person shall immediately report the suspicion and the information on which it is based to a society: *for a complete list of reporting reasons, please reference the CYFSA directly in s.125(1)*

s.125(3) Person must report directly – A person who has a duty to report a matter under subsection (1) or (2) shall make the report directly to the society and shall not rely on any other person to report on the person's behalf.

CHILDREN'S LAW REFORM ACT (CLRA, R.S.O. 1990):

s.20(4) Duty of separated parents – Where the parents of a child live separate & apart & the child lives with one of them with the consent, implied consent or acquiescence of the other of them, the right of the other to exercise the entitlement of custody & the incidents of custody, but not the entitlement to access, is suspended until a separation agreement or order otherwise provides.

s.20(5) Access – The entitlement to access to a child includes the right to visit with & be visited by the child & the same right as a parent to make inquiries & to be given information as to the health, education & welfare of the child.

DIVORCE ACT (R.S.C. 1985):

s.2(2) Child of the marriage – For the purposes of the definition "child of the marriage" in subsection (1), a child of two spouses or former spouses includes
    (a) any child for whom they both stand in the place of parents; and
    (b) any child of whom one is the parent and for whom the other stands in the place of a parent.

FAMILY LAW ACT (R.S.O. 1990):

s.3(3) Duty of mediator – The mediator shall confer with the parties, and with the children if the mediator considers it appropriate to do so, and shall endeavour to obtain an agreement between the parties. R.S.O. 1990, c. F.3, s. 3 (3).

s.13.1 Order regarding conduct – In making any order under this Part, the court may also make an interim order prohibiting, in whole or in part, a party from directly or indirectly contacting or communicating with another party, if the court determines that the order is necessary to ensure that an application under this Part is dealt with justly. 2009, c. 11, s. 27.

s.30 Obligation of spouses for support – Every spouse has an obligation to provide support for himself or herself and for the other spouse, in accordance with need, to the extent that he or she is capable of doing so. R.S.O. 1990, c. F.3, s. 30; 1999, c. 6, s. 25 (3); 2005, c. 5, s. 27 (7).

FAMILY RESPONSIBILITY & SUPPORT ARREARS ENFORCEMENT ACT:

s.10(1) Support deduction orders to be made – An Ontario court that makes a support order, as defined in subsection 1(1), shall also make a support deduction order.

s.23(1) Maximum deduction by income source – The total amount deducted by an income source and paid to the Director under a support deduction order shall not exceed 50 per cent of the net amount owed by the income source to the payor.

REFERENCES

Arbitration Act of 1991, S.O., (2017).

Beer, J.E., & Stief, E.(1997). The mediator's handbook (3rd ed.). Gabriola Island, British Columbia: New Society Publishers.

Bennett, M.D., & Hermann, M.S.G. (1996). The art of mediation. Notre Dame, Indiana: National Institute for Trial Advocacy.

Brown, P. (2013). Kosho shorei ryu of northumberland county curriculum (2nd ed.).

Clarke, A. (2017, September 22). Culture, power & diversity. Presented at Four Counties Family Court Mediation Services Roster Meeting.

Child and Family Services Act of 1990, R.S.O., (2016).

Children's Law Reform Act of 1990, R.S.O., (2017).

Child, Youth and Family Services Act of 2017, S.O.

Convery, P., King, M., & McCarty, B. (2016). Openness adoption training. Ontario Association for Family Mediation.

Dienstmann, G. (2016) Scientific benefits of meditation - 76 things you might be missing out on.

Divorce Act of 1985, R.S.C., (2015).

Family Law Act of 1990, R.S.O., (2017).

Family Responsibility and Support Arrears Enforcement Act of 1996, R.S.O., (2016).

Freedom of Information and Protection of Privacy Act of 1990, R.S.O., (2017).

George Hull Centre. (2011). Family group conferencing/ family group decision making coordinator manual for ontario. Ontario, Canada: The George Hull Centre.

Halmasy, N. (2016). After the call: Mental health awareness for families of first responders.

Heintz, M. (2012). Study outline: Version 20120122.

Hole, J.W., Jr (1992). Essentials of human anatomy & physiology (4th ed.). Dubuque, IA: Wm. C. Brown Publishers.

http://www.canadacourtwatch.com

http://www.children.gov.on.ca

http://www.compassionfatigue.org

http://www.cpmed.ca

http://dictionary.cambridge.org

http://www.lfcc.on.ca

http://www.mayoclinic.com

http://www.oacas.org

http://psychologytoday.com

http://www.riverdalemediation.com

http://www.socialworkdegreeguide.com

http://www.torontocas.ca

http://www.un.org

http://www.yourdictionary.com/mediation

http://www.ammsa.com/node/12407

https://www.attorneygeneral.jus.gov.on.ca

https://www.ccpa-accp.ca

Indian Act of 1985, R.S.C., (2015).

Jaffe, P. (2017, May 17). Preventing domestic homicides. Presented at Family Group Conferencing Ontario Provincial Resource Professional Development Day. PowerPoint retrieved May 18, 2017 from Centre for Research & Education on Violence Against Women & Children.

Landau, B. (2008). Domestic violence screening and practice skills. Cooperative Solutions.

Lomax, J. (2017, May 17). Adoption ceremony. Presented at Family Group Conferencing Ontario Provincial Resource Professional Development Day.

Maresca, J.A., Hall, M., & Chornenki, G.A. (2006). Child protection mediation: an introductory course. Ontario Ministry of Children and Youth Services.

Ministry of Children and Youth Services. (2016). Ontario child welfare eligibility spectrum (Rev. ed.).

Office of the Chief Coroner. (2016). Inquest touching the death of Katelynn Sampson; Jury verdict and recommendations. Toronto, ON: Queen's Printer of Ontario.

Orloff, J. (2011). Emotional freedom: Liberate yourself from negative emotions and transform your life. New York: Three Rivers Press.

Patzner, C. & DeCook, K. (2017, October 18). Widening the circle. Presented at International Conference on Innovations in Family Engagement.

Schuman, J.P. (2012). Guide to the basics of ontario family law. (3rd ed.). Devry Smith & Frank LLP.

Saini, M. (2017, September 21). Precious voices - Authentic involvement of children in child protection mediation with families involved in high conflict. Presented at Blue Hills Child & Family Centre Annual Joint Roster Meeting.

Paul Brown Mediation
PO Box 21016
1875 Lansdowne St W
Peterborough, ON Canada
K9J 8M7

www.ingramcontent.com/pod-product-compliance
Lightning Source LLC
Chambersburg PA
CBHW071411170526
45165CB00001B/244